Judge Dee plays his lute:
a play and selected mystery stories

by
Janwillem van de Wetering

Wonderly Press   Bar Harbor, Maine   1997

Copyright © 1997 Janwillem van de Wetering
All rights reserved.

ISBN(limited edition): 0-9660927-2-4
ISBN(trade hardback): 0-9660927-0-8
ISBN(trade paperback): 0-9660927-1-6

FIRST EDITION
10 9 8 7 6 5 4 3 2 1

Wonderly Press
Dunn and Powell Books
The Hideaway
Bar Harbor, ME 04609
U. S. A.

For Barbara Peters

Contents

Introduction -- 1

The Flower Print Murder -- 5

The Queen's Angel -- 23

Happy Hermits --- 37

Non-Interference -- 57

A Law Student -- 91

Off Season -- 111

Inspector Saito and the Twenty-Sen Stamp ---------------- 119

Trumpetbird in the Cop Car ---------------------------------- 135

The Murders in the Alley of the Mad Nun ---------------- 145

Judge Dee Plays His Lute -------------------------------------- 157

INTRODUCTION

Nobody I know ever reads introductions; but some folks, I'm told, may glance at that separate first page after they have read what the introduction aims to refer to. So on the off-chance that any dear reader partakes of these words on the backlash, I project these words on a back-lit screen:

The play JUDGE DEE PLAYS HIS LUTE was suggested to me during a lecture tour in Germany. A completely hairless-headed man in impeccable three-piece attire said "you should write a play."
"A what?" I looked stupid and he explained.
"Sure. A radioplay. It could be performed in my cinema. How would you like that?"
As he looked, even sounded serious, I suggested we go out to eat fried flounder (Hamburg is just the place for that) and he explained further. Radioplays are quite popular in Germany, for listening to on the Autobahn, at speed.
"So what kind of a play?" I asked. "Crime?" and he said Crime was good but that he preferred hallucinations, mysticism, the spiritual path and messing up on same. Evidently he knew my work for these are subjects dear to my heart. I said I would see what I could do.
It didn't take that long. The next year the play was to be performed on Nord Deutsche Radio but before that my wife and I were invited to a small cinema in Hamburg, one Sunday morning. The venue was sold out, there was a strange breathless quality to the silence of the audience, but I still didn't get it. A radio-play in a cinema? Was everybody mad?
There was jazz on the sound system, Miles Davis' "SO WHAT?"
The tune came to an end. The curtains opened slowly and on stage stood a straight-up chair with on its seat an old-fashioned radio-set, appearing small, pitiful, inefficient.
What the hell? But then a circus director appeared on stage, a

man with a belly and a goatee and high spit-polish boots. The apparition wore a frock coat, riding breeches, marched up to the chair, extended a meaningful hand, and switched on the tiny set with an elegant long finger.

Immediately wrap-around sound filled the theatre. The play burst upon us. A city burst into flame. Motorcycles roared. Lovers kissed in the surf behind an African beach. The huge swish of the unshaven Zen monk's ink-dipped broom drawing a black zero on a sheet sparked colorful imagination. The feet of nude young women tripping on the hardwood floor around Dr. van Gulik's coffin were respectfully erotic.

As for the stories:

"Happy Hermits" was inspired by a bizarre accident I witnessed on the A1A, some ten miles south of Key West. "Drunken Killer-Driver escapes into the Mangroves". It was Christmas time. The sort of event one cannot afford not to write.

"The Queen's Angel" is a rewritten psychiatric report found in the venerable writings of Carl Jung.

"Non-Interference" started as a "commercial." A Dutch manufacturer had come out with a "beeper" and an advertising agent suggested a tale to advertise the product in a leaflet.

"Trumpetbird in the Cop Car" comes from my years with the Amsterdam Constabulary and is uncomfortably close to most actually, even intimately, witnessed facts. There was, indeed, a bad man like Fastbuck Freddie, accompanied by "his" beautiful and abused stripper. Even the noisy bird was there.

Again, "The Flowerprint Murder" is not imagined. I was a "rider" in a Maine sheriff's cruiser when the deputy at the wheel mentioned a woman's corpse, found on the beach that day. The case obsessed me and I got to follow it, step by grisly step, until the killer was apprehended.

"Off Season" dates back to a "beatnik" period in Japan, late fifties. The search for truth. There were others, looking too.

"A Law Student" goes back to Amsterdam again, and the rise of escort agencies linked to organized crime, a novelty in the sixties.

"Inspector Saito and the Twenty-Sen Stamp" combines a long-gone interest in stamp collecting with a still-present penchant for unraveling exotic puzzles.

    Odd writings for your perusal, published, as a limited edition, by a respected Catalogue distributing rare books. An instantly-rare collector's item. May the book amuse you.

                                           Janwillem van de Wetering
                                           Surry, Maine
                                           September 1997

The Flower Print Murder

Deputy Sheriff Champlain sat back on the deck he'd built off his trailer and watched the sunrise. The first of the chickadees began to flit between Champlain's feeders, some set on posts, some hanging from nearby trees. The birds' cheerful, simple little songs counterpointed the memory of cacophonies that drove Champlain from a comfortable bed to exposure beneath cold, fading stars. Gunfire had been in the dream, and the ground around him erupting from incoming grenades. There were the screams of platoon mates as they fell around him. And all the while medic Champlain walked calmly, upright, unscathed beneath his Red Cross helmet, to return safely while his buddies died. The dream was based on real, random survival. Champlain should not be alive now. The Viet Cong liked to aim at medics first.

Other birds joined the friendly chickadees. Purple finches, a small tribe of juncos, a pair of song sparrows chased by blue jays kept returning. The cries of the jays mixed with the smaller birds' chirping created a not unpleasing medley that lulled the deputy into a doze that lasted a good two hours, then was shattered when his phone rang inside the trailer.

He got up from his hard cane couch, stretched, went inside. "Yeah?"

"Rise and shine, Champ."

It was Sheriff Sipock. Champlain was supposed to be on early duty that spring day, to relieve Sipock, who would be off to breakfast in the kitchen adjoining his office.

"You up, Champ?"

"Aimlessly afloat in an empty universe," Champlain said. "Sorry." His eyes scanned the spotless interior of the trailer. Even his unmade bed, the sheets folded back with mathematical precision, looked neat. It was hard to reconcile his orderly bachelor lodgings with the recurring dream's violent chaos. "Anything up?"

"You ain't missed much so far," said Sipock. "You think you might be coming now, Old Buddy? Not feeling bad again?"

"Dreams," Champlain said. "But I'm up and about now."

"Share an omelet" the sheriff asked. "Like the one you cook?

With spinach? Kiwis and cream to follow?"

"Kiwis?" Champlain held the phone at some distance.

"Don't rightly know what kiwis might be," Sipock admitted. He chuckled. "Live and learn. There was a *New Yorker* cartoon in Dentist Cary's office showing a sign in a restaurant window that said: 'Will not serve kiwis.' A fruit of some sort?"

"Pippy and sour," Champlain said. "Acquired taste. Join you in a minute. Betty isn't home for the weekend?"

"Betty," Sipock said. "Would that be some sort of woman?"

"On my way," Champlain said. He was dressing as he talked. He and Sipock went back a few years now, helping to maintain harmony along the wild coast and within the wetlands of Woodcock County, Maine. Betty Sipock, the sheriff's wayward wife, no longer cared for "the desolation." Betty would go off to work in her Bostonian sister's Fusion Dance Studio and attend spiritual workshops where she met men who shared. Betty wasn't home too often now.

Champlain knew Sipock's tone of voice, and its subtle fluctuations. Listening to his superior's grating, wheezy words, he reckoned something had happened, nothing serious though. Sheriff Sipock wouldn't normally call his deputy if the latter was late.

"Nothing is up?" Champlain asked. "It's too early, right? Too Sunday?"

"Just Preacher Pooter on the blower," Sipock said. "Old buzzard has been doing his rounds, as always on Lordy days, waving the Holy Book, and Christina LaCroix won't open the door of her cabin on Neck Road. Pooter has been hollering and kicking and whistling. No go. Mind checking with Christina on your way up? Pooter sounded kinda worried. Hard to get him off the phone. I would go, but Tom hasn't showed yet."

Tom was Woodcock County's part-time dispatcher, part-time homesteader, not too punctual an official either.

"Old Miss LaCroix?" Champlain asked, putting on his gunbelt. "Isn't she one of the believers? Why wouldn't she let Preacher Pooter in?"

"Some believe opposite," Sipock said. "Maybe Preach gets a little too pushy?"

Keith Jarrett's Cologne Concert sounded from the cruiser's

tapeplayer as Champlain, driving south on Barberry Neck Road, followed the county's spectacular shore. The deputy, lips pursed, head slightly to the side, enjoyed the music as he glanced at white breakers rolling along a purple granite ledge. He passed several small coves where winter ducks still dived for mussels before turning the cruiser into Christina LaCroix's driveway. The driveway was marked with low walls of fieldstones, partly overgrown with dry silver moss. He parked behind the old lady's rustbucket Oldsmobile. He smiled. He could imagine the indignant rage it would kindle in Pooter to be ignored by rightful prey. Champlain had been treated to Pooter's visitations too, once while he was renovating his trailer, just after he bought it, when it still showed signs of psychopathic occupation. After fixing the outside, he'd torn out all partitions and was burning scrap when the white-bearded man with long stringy hair approached from the fire's off-side. Pooter could pass for an Old Testament apparition, certainly that time. One vengeful prophet, framed by flames.

"Saw the fumes and knew it must be one of God's lost lambs smoking," Pooter hollered, holding up a large tattered Bible and shaking a poplar branch.

Champlain, from his days in New York's Greenwich Village, had some experience in dealing with the savior fringe. He threw out his arms. "I've been *waiting*." He pointed at glowing coals. "Step right up, step right *UP*."

Pooter, shaken from his routine by Champlain dancing toward him, changed modes. Coastal cynicism overcame Puritan ideals. "Maryjane?" Pooter asked pleasantly. "Any good grass to spare, me lad?"

"The weed," Champlain said, "no longer works for me."

Pooter stuck his staff in the ground, skipped around the fire, and peered into Champlain's face. "Ain't you Pete Champlain's boy?" He prodded the deputy's chest. "Yes, I see the likeness. You must be what became of little Christof." He shook his Bible in Chaplain's face. Weren't you the one who played with cut-out dolls as a kid? Got your father all worried?" Pooter caressed his beard, shaking his head. "Sorry to hear what happened to the old ones." Pooter scowled. "I dunno, me lad, even if ye're both real old, even if ye're both real sick, faith will prevail." He dropped his voice. "A handgun, was it?"

Champlain shrugged.

Pooter preached then, after stepping behind flames again. "Let us purify ourselves, leave the Sodom of our minds."

Champlain, using a long-stemmed spade, stirred the fire. He thought of Vietnamese Buddhist monks pouring gasoline on their heads, then burning while they sat, their legs locked in the lotus position.

Pooter prayed, then lifted his torn straw hat.

Blessings, dear." He smiled kindly. "You back for good? Had enough of city sin?"

"Yes," Champlain said sincerely. There was some contact between them then, kept up through the years by wobbled eyebrows when their cars met on the road between Sorry and Rotworth. As Sheriff Sipock said: "No reason to be rude. We're all mad anyway."

As he walked to the cabin's front door, Champlain looked to see if there was smoke coming out of Christina's brick chimney. There wasn't any, but on a nice spring morning like this the old lady might well have let the fire die. He knocked. While waiting, he admired forsythia bushes flanking the front door. The yellow flowers were bright and cheery. He knocked again, calling Christina's name, identifying himself so she'd know he wasn't the dreaded Pooter. "Sheriff's office. How are you doing, Miz LaCroix?"

The cabin just sat there. The deputy, neatly uniformed, boots and gunbelt creaking, his Stetson set at the prescribed police school angle, walked around the building to where Christina was starting her vegetable garden for the season. Nothing to be alarmed about, he thought. Friends probably picked the old thing up for church, Humanitarian Chapel most likely. The lady might be planning to have lunch afterward, at the Lighthouse Inn, looking across the channel toward Ropeshoe Island. Hope to see a finback whale cruise by. Drink decaf from pink porcelain cups. Eat blueberry pancakes. The Sunday outing.

Champlain wondered what Pooter could be upset about. Was this an instance of the prophet's uncanny insight?

Looking across junipers growing along Christina's property line, he noticed a small bright-green car sitting behind the house of Christina's neighbor. The deputy recalled Mr. Bollinger was a live-alone too. He briefly visualized the image of Clarence Bollinger, a small, dainty man who owned the health food store in nearby Sorry. Champlain had met

Bollinger at Sorry Post Office, where the store owner, talking about the deficit with the postmaster and fellow clients, claimed to be a buy-American man. Earlier on, when Champlain came back from Viet Nam in a bemedaled uniform, Clarence had stepped forward on Main Street and doffed his hat. "We're proud of you, young man. I want you to know that."

Must be lightening up a bit, thought Champlain. The little green car was a Subaru, a "tin roller skate," as Bollinger had called Japanese imports. Champlain didn't recall ever having seen Bollinger drive the compact. As far as he knew, Clarence drove a Dodge full-size pickup.

Champlain drove to work, after stopping at the Sorry General Store.

"Morning," Sheriff Sipock said. He smiled at a paper bag filled with omelet ingredients that Champlain carried in. Sipock, firmly stuck to his swivel chair, rolled across to the coffee machine in the near corner of his kitchen "Don't strain yourself, Champ. I need the exercise. Java Mocha. Got it for you out of a catalogue. Kinda like it myself."

Champlain chuckled. The sheriff was the county's fat man. Sipock, locally known as Sixpack, managed his jurisdiction with less attention to law than to the remote area's peculiar sense of harmony and justice. For revenue Sipock preferred to use the summer people. "Caught myself three Volvos and a Mercedes speeding this week, now you bag us a bunch of BMWs, Champ." Winter was best spent sitting around the Franklin stove, sucking Cuban cigars donated by a Colombian skipper stuck on Hangman's Rock while watching ten tons of imports float off into the Atlantic.

Sipock mostly cared for Betty's goats, which Betty herself had long ago lost interest in. Sipock liked to milk the wily creatures. He sold the milk profitably to a Portland firm canning the product as part of an anti-allergy diet.

"I delegate crime, therefore I milk," he would tell Number One Goat Margarita. Crime detection was the deputy's realm. Crime, according to the sheriff, was city-inpired, best taken care of by experts. Champlain, after Viet Nam, had spent ten years in New York. "Besides," Sipock told Margarita, "being usefully engaged helps the young feller handle those interesting dreams."

"Besides," Sipock whispered into Margarita's downy ear, "why work if you don't have to?"

The sheriff now slid along on squeaky ball bearings and passed a steaming mug to Champlain. "You bring any frozen crew-sants?"

Champlain had brought oven-fresh biscuits.

"How crude," Sipock said. "Here I'm trying to get educated. You talk to old lady LaCroix on the way?"

Champlain worked on the omelet. "Her car was there but she wasn't. I figure she got picked up by her sewing circle. Church time, you know."

Sipock interrupted his noisy swallowing, caused by watching the omelet rise. "Not holed up in her attic hiding from the hollering prophet?"

"I hollered too," Champlain said. "Not a sign of Christina. Preacher Pooter being cantankerous again? Causing trouble?"

Sipock tried to look away from the stove where Champlain's special mixture of vegetables and mushrooms simmered in a separate pot. "Maybe we ought to lean on Pooter a bit. Been driving that old pickup without a sticker for how long now? And his deer-chasing mutt without a tag? Growing Maryjane behind his chapel?"

The phone rang. Champlain, having served the omelets, took the call. It was Clarence Bollinger wondering if the deputy sheriff was aware of any trouble at the LaCroix residence.

"Saw me, did you?" Champlain asked. "Christina didn't come to the door. You have any cause to worry, sir?" He pressed the phone's speaker button. Sipock, able to listen in now, grunted thanks.

Clarence Bollinger was, being a good neighbor, concerned about Christina not answering her door when he came over that morning after he saw the deputy leave. Bollinger explained that ever since former bank-teller Christina retired, he kept an eye on the old spinster. The day before, Saturday, on the phone, Christina mentioned not feeling too well. He had brought her some groceries. Her car was right there. He had phoned but she didn't pick up.

"Church?" Champlain asked. "Someone picked her up?"

"Could be," Bollinger said. "Yes, perhaps. There has been a lady calling on her lately, she said. Didn't see the lady myself. Could be. I'll see if she comes back."

"Let us know if she doesn't," Champlain said. "Thank you for reporting this, sir."

"Much afuss about niffink," Sipock said when the deputy broke the connection. Sheriff Sipock wasn't worried enough not to eat his omelet. He persuaded Champlain to sit down and join him. "What are the mushrooms?"

"You like them?" Champlain said, his fork raised. Sipock looked dubious.

"Grew them in the trailer," Champlain said. "Dried them myself. I wanted to try them out on you. So they are good?"

Sipock shuddered.

Champlain laughed. "They're okay. Shitaki. A staple in Japan. Japanese are fussy eaters." He put mushrooms into his mouth, hewed, swallowed. "See?"

"Maybe," Sipock said, "Christina had cabin fever." He gestured as if warding off bad spirits. "What with the weather we been having? This morning it was nice for the first time in a week. Christina skipped church and went for a walk instead? On the beach? Walks sort of bent over, because of her bad backbone? She slipped off a boulder? You want to check that sometime, Champ?"

Champlain, half his omelet left and swallowed by Sipock the minute the cruiser's engine started up, returned to Neck Road. Be noticed crows flying up and circling near the Neck's pebble beach. There was an eagle too, white tail and head clearly visible. "Seal," Champlain thought. He had seen a few lately. Dying or dead seals attract crows and eagles. He drove for another minute, then U-turned abruptly, drove back. During the war scavenger birds often led him to missing soldiers. Champlain wasn't surprised now when he saw the grave, or what passed for a grave. The shallow hole might have been dug by hand, in a desperate hurry. Pebbles and small rocks were pushed across the body. Christina's arms stuck out. Her hands seemed to be beckoning the crows that hopped and fluttered use by. One shoulder was already exposed by digging birds. The flowerprint pattern on the dress, white and red roses on a yellow background, was stained with dried blood.

Champlain walked back to the cruiser and raised Sipock. Sipock raised the state police. A detective helicoptered in within hours and immediately fenced off the area with metal rods and yellow tape. Later a photographer arrived, a medical young lady from the capital's coroner's office, more state police, the county hearse, three reporters who, with other curious folks, were kept at distance by Sipock and Champlain until volunteer constables from Sorry and Rotworth came to replace the sheriffs.

Preacher Pooter's beat-up white jeep, decorated with handpainted black crosses, was spotted late that afternoon, almost in the next county, from the state-police helicopter, with Champlain pointing down. The chopper landed. "I'm doing Lordy work," Pooter said. "You can't bother me now."

The state detective was polite. "Just some questions, Mr. Pooter, sir. You called this morning; we're curious—the lady you called about is dead, you see, murdered."

Pooter denied all knowledge of beating Christina about the head with her own baseball bat (signed by Ted Williams; Christina claimed the signature was real, but it was printed, of course) kept behind her door for the last thirty years. The bat, blood spattered, was found in the house. The handle had been wiped clean.

"You weren't in the house?"

"Never," Pooter said.

Christina's skull was broken in several places. The medical young lady thought the violence had been committed that very morning, early, daybreak maybe.

"Can we print your shoes?" the detective asked.

Pooter would not take off his shoes. He claimed an amendment. He became more and more upset.

"In that case, you'll have to come with me," the detective said gently.

"In that machine?" Pooter asked, aghast.

The old man was whisked off into the sky. Champlain drove the jeep back to Sorry.

Sipock was tending his goats when Champlain came back. The sheriff walked to the office. While coffee perked, Sipock theorized. "Got ourselves a killer?" He constructed a hypothesis while the deputy listened, making sure known facts fitted. "Look," Sipock said. "We know

Pooter preys on the innocents Sundays and can get mighty obstreperous when thwarted. State detective ascertained that Pooter's shoeprints matched the prints left around victim's house. Suspect's guilty conscience made him nervous when you guys stopped him. Wouldn't have his shoes printed. Wasn't that suspicious? Fugitive was almost out of the county by the time officers tracked him down. Pooter is known for temper. Christina was wearing this newfangled non-Christian flowerprint dress. Pooter didn't like that. You should have heard him holler."

"Flowerprint dress?" Champlain asked. "You showed him the corpse just now?"

"That flowerprint dress made Pooter extraordinarily anxious," Sipock said. "Called it a 'sinful outfit.'"

Sipock acted out the possible murder scene. Here is Preacher Pooter being let in by his sister in the faith, Christina LaCroix, on Neck Road, a woman he has known all his life, whom he went through school with. Pooter means well at first. Christina does believe, but not too rightly yet. There need to be some improvements, and Pooter is qualified to administer same, but now what happens? Christina claims that her mealy-mouthed, watered-down, slippery excuse for true faith is essentially superior to Pooter's fire and brimstone. Preacher Pooter is aghast. He grabs this flowerprinted sinner and yells there are neither either nor ors. Only Pooter's brand is guaranteed. Christina loses her temper, tries to shove the spiritual bully to the door. The baseball bat happens to be around. She picks it up. Pooter wrestles the weapon away from her.

"Right?" Sipock stopped in front of his deputy. Champlain noticed that the sheriff was sweating, trembling, panting. "Right, Champ?" Sipock bellowed.

Champlain pushed out his lower lip and waved his right hand, palm up. Sipock refused to acknowledge the mimed objection. Sipock moved his bulk around Champlain's chair, swinging the invisible murder weapon. "Bam bam BAM!"

The sheriff was panting. "Yes?"

"Nah," Champlain said.

The sheriff, out of breath, fell into his swivel chair.

"That's what the detective said." Sipock pointed at Champlain's seat. "He had Pooter right there, then let him go. No bail. Dropped Pooter off even, in a state cruiser. Promised you would return the jeep pronto." Sipock's heavy eyebrows curved lower. "You figure why the suspect was let go, Champ?"

"Pooter denies guilt," Champlain said. No reason not to believe him. The footprints around the house mean nothing. Pooter said he walked around the cabin, when he phoned you. Remember? Can't hold a fellow citizen for not liking to take his shoes off."

"If you say so," Sipock said, shaking his head. "*If* you say so."

Champlain took pity on the sweating fat man. "What else happened, Sip?"

"Not much." Sipock shrugged. "More about that flowerprint dress. Hell and damnation. I thought Pooter would lose it. Man was frothing."

"Pooter was never too stable," Champlain said.

Sipock snorted. "Mad as a rabid coon." He looked up. "You tired? Mind sniffing Pooter again? You got to return his jeep anyway. Give me a call when you're done sniffing. Provided Tom is back from feeding his chickens, I'll come pick you up."

"Sniffing Pooter for what?" Champlain asked.

Sheriff Sipock looked unhappy. "It's that flowerprint dress Christina wore that riles me. Riles Pooter too. There's something there. I *know* it."

Champlain found Pooter at the little chapel the preacher had built himself on the Neck Road. There was a sign: PREACHER POOTER'S NONDENOMINATIONAL CHURCH, and, in small letters, *all Protestants welcome*. The deputy found Pooter at the top of a ladder, prying a rotten board off the roof. The preacher threatened Champlain with his hammer. "Can't have my shoes again. You git. You hear?"

"Just returning your jeep," Champlain said. He pointed at the chapel's lopsided spire. "Nice design, you're truly artistic, Preach. Bless the Lord."

Pooter, mollified, holstered his hammer before climbing down.

"Wonder what Christina was doing on the beach today?" Champlain asked. "Collecting treasures?"

Pooter laughed grimly. "Water scared Chrissie silly. Could never get her skinny-dipping when we was kids."

"What?" Champlain asked. "*Naked*, you mean? You and Chris-

14

tina? You suggested she take her clothes off?"

"*Kids*." Pooter held a hand a foot off the ground to indicate his and Christina's early sizes. "Before we knew no better."

"And she wouldn't go near water?"

"Hated the shore," Pooter said. "Scared her. Only lived there because she got the house off her folks." He scowled. "Must have dragged her there, Sheriff."

"Who, Preach?"

"Mr. Devil." Pooter almost reached for his hammer but seemed restrained by Champlain's uniform and gunbelt. "She surrendered herself." Pooter bent forward and whispered meaningfully, "Thou shalt not worship false gods, or in unbecoming attire."

"Flowerprint dress?" Champlain asked.

"Flowerprint dress," Pooter affirmed solemnly. "I told her what to do often enough. 'Don't cut your hair, go barefoot, wear long dark cloth. Repent. Bless your Sundays.'" He took a deep breath. "But NOOOOO!" Pooter's eyes bulged as he stared at Champlain. "So then what happens?"

Champlain stepped back. "You told her that, eh?"

"Again and again. Right in her own home. I'd come calling. Doing Lordy work. Talking my teeth down to the gums. Reclaiming the lost ones." The preacher glowered. "Doing my best, right until Mr. Devil claims her."

"But you didn't see her today?"

"Christina wasn't home," Pooter said. "Her car was. Strange, don't you think?" Pooter suddenly seemed quite normal. He offered the deputy cashew nuts from a can that he fetched from his hiding place behind the pulpit. He called in Nehemiah, a scarred pitbull terrier that sat up and grinned after touching Champlain's right hand respectfully with her paw. The two men discussed bird feeding and Pooter mentioned unusual birds that were coming round that spring. A cardinal. An oriole. Pooter and Champlain practiced birdcalls together.

"Amazing," Sheriff Sipock said, after picking Champlain up. "You have a gift there, Champ. You should try it on my goats sometime. Fancy getting Pooter to talk normal to you."

"Like Pooter has a second personality?" the young state detective asked after hearing Champlain's report next day. The detective had spent Sunday night and Monday morning checking the crime site and the grave. He had invited sheriff and deputy for dinner in the inn where he was staying. He addressed Sipock. "You grew up with Pooter. What was he like at school? Any bullying, beating up, displays of sadism?"

Sipock, slicing an oversize steak, shook his head.

"Pooter wasn't on the beach," the detective said. "Unless he was wearing female shoes, high-heeled, half his size. We did find tracks of those. Just a few, where the body was dragged off ledge into gravel, where it was buried later on."

"Multiple personalities," Sipock said, while waiting for more, fries. "We all have them. Some better, some worse. Odd little things seem to trigger them off. You should meet Betty." The sheriff grimaced. "My wife. One of her lesser personalities, that doesn't get triggered off too often, is quite pleasant."

"Flowerprint," Champlain said, "triggers off Pooter's bad side?"

Sheriff Sipock stopped eating. "Flowerprint, absolutely. Now there's a trigger. I have been dreaming of blood-spattered flowerprinted dresses all night. Sexy. Forbidding." Sipock was sweating, gesturing with his steak knife. "Frightening. Fascinating."

"Don't get it," the detective said. "The phenomenon sure gets you guys going. Pooter." He looked at the sheriff. "You too." He looked at Champlain. "Something local maybe? It excites you too?"

Champlain shook his head. "What's so sexy about flowerprint dresses? Seem rather stodgy to me. Frumpish even."

"*You* tell us," the detective asked Sipock. "You say you dreamed all night? Nightmares? Flowery visions?"

"By the way," Sipock said. "You mentioned Christina had been robbed as well. Her pocketbook was empty?"

The state detective said the theft might not mean much. Killing and theft often go together. Once the victim is down, possessions are taken. He didn't think theft was a special motivation here. "Flowerprint," the detective said. "Mind answering my question, Sheriff? What's with the flowerprint dress? Why does that make you and Pooter sweat and stammer?"

Sipock was sweating again. He said he didn't know.

"Help me, Sheriff."

"I'm trying, Detective."

Champlain finally scored first. Sheriff and preacher, Champlain pointed out, were the same age. When the two were in puberty, times were sexually restricted. "Repressed," the detective said. "Sexual hangups," Champlain said. "We still have them here somewhat."

Sipock laughed. "Somewhat a lot, especially with folks my age. You're right there, Champ. You think there's a sexual connotation? Flowerprint—hanky-panky?"

"Keep going," the state detective said.

"Okay," Sipock nodded. "I understand my dream better now. For me and Preacher Pooter the flowerprint fashion arrives second time around. The first time it hit harder."

"Pubertal guilt feelings aroused by flowerprint dresses in males in their late fifties," the detective said. "I'll write a paper on that, should help out with my graduate studies. I thank you, Sheriff."

"Details?" Champlain asked.

Sipock had grown up with several adult sisters, and youngish aunts. They wore flowerprint dresses when he became sexually conscious, fifty years ago. He desired those women, in the way they looked then.

"Did you want to wear flowerprint dresses yourself?" Champlain asked.

"Please," Sipock said. "Isn't desiring my sisters bad enough? That's incestuous. That's why I couldn't come up with an immediate answer." Sipock blushed.

"Seems to me we're looking for a perverted perpetrator here," the state detective said. "Someone male presumably, seeing that the corpse got carried quite some distance. Not Pooter, who wears size fourteen. A male with small feet who likes to dress up as a female and wear high-heeled shoes. Maybe likes to wear flowerprint dresses too. A transvestite who is homicidal when wearing a flowerprint dress, especially when his opponent, presumed opponent, wears another?"

"Switch of character," Sipock said. "Like the postmaster here. He's okay when he drives his mini-van, but he goes nuts when he rides his Harley."

Champlain almost jumped. "Japanese compact versus a full-size, all-American pickup? Okay one way, not at all okay the other? Or the other way around?"

"Right," the detective said. "You have a suspect now?"

"Let me do a little work here." Champlain got up. "Thanks for a great dinner. See you at your office, sheriff. I might come up with something. I'll phone you here at the inn, Detective."

Clarence Bollinger looked relieved when he saw Champlain on his porch. "Come in, deputy, such doings! Poor Christina. That helicopter was certainly busy. All of you were, weren't you?"

The two men sat in Bollinger's living room, with a wide view of Bunker Bay; beautiful, Champlain thought—four brown sails of the first tourist schooner of the season under wispy sunset-tinted clouds. He was comfortable in a large overstuffed easy chair upholstered with clean linen. He liked Bollinger's flower arrangements. He praised an enormous painting above the fireplace that showed a semi-nude woman on a couch. The woman could be forty. She was biting into an apple. There was a dog in the painting too, a large Labrador with its mouth open. Its long narrow pink tongue hung out. The woman's large but firm breasts, exposed by a flowerprint dress (red and white roses on a yellow background) sliding off pink shoulders, had different sizes. The woman seemed happy, unaware she was having her portrait painted.

The dog had its paws on the woman's lap and was pulling down her dress.

"Aunt Louisa and Christina the dog," Clarence Bollinger said. "Those two raised me. In New York. I was born here in Rotworth but my parents died in an accident, so Aunt Louisa took me over. She died last month, in her late seventies. The attorney sent me the painting. It's only been up a few weeks. You like it?"

Champlain tried to smile. He didn't like the painting so much now. It seemed indecent to him, sadistic. Both woman and dog smirked. Christina? Same name as the dead neighbor?

Clarence Bollinger, questioned by the deputy, seemed genuinely hurt by neighbor Christina's murder.

Was, Champlain asked, the little car outside Aunt Louisa's?

Bollinger was all smiles. Very helpful. Yes, he had inherited Aunt Louisa's car too, the green Subaru that he had just gotten Maine plates for, and Aunt's clothes, yes, everything. The dog Christina was long dead, of course. Talking of Christina, would the deputy mind filling Bollinger in re Christina LaCroix's murder?

So Christina was killed with a baseball bat. Awful. And her purse was emptied of money. Horrifying. A thief? Bollinger kept shaking his head, clasping and unclasping his hands. His eyes were wet.

The man must be working out, Champlain thought, remembering having seen weights in the corridor and a fitness machine. Bollinger might be small, but he was athletic. Close to sixty but in great shape. Close to sixty, same age as Pooter and Sheriff Sipock.

The deputy asked Clarence whether he, the caring, ever aware neighbor, had noticed anything out of the ordinary lately? In Christina's murder there seemed to have been a woman involved. "Know of any lady visitors, Clarence?"

Bollinger desperately studied Champlain's face. "I guess you've seen plenty of this sort of thing, Deputy. Between Viet Nam and New York. Blood and gore. Was it police work you were doing in the Big Apple?"

Why not? Champlain thought. Reaching out, getting personal, might help. He told Clarence Bollinger how he, Champlain, was the lone survivor in a Viet Nam battle, just before coming back. Eighteen men down, the bullets somehow missed medic Christof Champlain. How, back in Sorry, his parents worried about his lack of interest in girls. How he became a handyman in New York. How, with pals, he restored and sold a building in Tribeca.

"Pals," Bollinger said. He bit the nail off his index finger. "In Tribeca?"

"They died," Champlain said. "Three down. The virus somehow missed me."

"Back to Sorry again," Bollinger said, studying his ripped fingernail. "I know where you live now. Didn't you restore that awful trailer and put up all those feeders, on Bayview Road? Cleaned up your woods? It looks lovely now, like a park. I like your cedar hedges."

"Really?" Champlain looked pleased. "You noticed?"

"The landscaping cheers me up when I drive by," Bollinger said. "Your bird feeders look like little pagodas. Picked that up in Viet Nam?"

Bollinger walked Champlain to the cruiser. The full moon, luminously golden yellow, topped a line of tall evergreens. Aunt Louisa's Subaru reflected the moon's rays.

"Hardly use that toy," Bollinger said. " Much prefer the Dodge. Still going strong after a hundred thousand."

Champlain drove the cruiser to the sheriffs office. On the way Wynona Judd sang "LUVVV" from a tape. Love is possessive, the deputy thought, often abusive. Clarence Bollinger was possessed by his nude aunt. Growing up with domineering human and canine females. A dog called Christina rips a dress off a lopsided mother/lover figure. A small frail boy watches.

The deputy remembered how Bollinger bit off a fingernail at the mention of Tribeca. 'Triangle Below Canal Street.' Not a good area. He remembered "Transvestite Square," where spectacular prostitutes postured in yellow lamplight.

"You two gentlemen apprehend Suspect," the detective said after Champlain reported. "You and I both know him. You're in uniform. It will lie better that way. I'll just make him nervous."

"At his house?" Sipock asked.

"Not necessarily." The detective shook his head. He looked out of the window. "Full moon tonight, that will be a factor. Suspect won't be able to sleep. You might find him outside. In drag. In the compact."

Sipock and Champlain checked the grave location first. There were raccoons on the ledge, partying on moonlit rocks, yapping and snarling. The lights were on in the Bollinger cottage and the Dodge pickup truck was parked in the driveway.

"He is home," Sipock said.

"*She* is not," Champlain said "Left in the Subaru, but where to? Might be anywhere by now." He waved at the radio. "Put out an APB?" Sipock didn't think so. The cruiser nosed along slowly, finding the Subaru a mile farther along, on a turn-out, scenic, created for tourists.

Champlain switched off the cruiser's engine. He and Sipock watched Bollinger toss dollar bills out of the compact's window. "Getting rid of the loot taken off Christina LaCroix," Sipock said. "Bollinger doesn't need the money. Can't remember why he took it. Wants us to arrest him. It's like throwing out party invitations."

The figure in the car became still. Champlain walked over. "Evening, dear. Like to come with us now?"

Bollinger, dressed in Aunt Louisa's flowerprint dress, and heavily made-up, took a small pistol from his lap. His hand trembled as he pointed it at his forehead.

"Better give that to me, dear," Champlain said.

The pistol pointed at Champlain's head now. The deputy put out his hand. Bollinger sighed, then handed over the gun.

"Thank you, dear." Champlain opened the Subaru's door. He walked, with Bollinger daintily stepping on high-heeled shoes and leaning on his arm, back to the cruiser.

"Aunt Louisa trained Christina to pull off that dress," Bollinger said in a high but natural-sounding voice, "and then she'd sic the dog, on me."

"How are you feeling?" Champlain asked.

"I have felt better," Bollinger said. "I'm very tired."

"You drive, Sheriff, please," Champlain said. "I'll sit in the back with our friend. Clarence is tired."

Bollinger smiled when Sipock reversed the cruiser from the turnout. His hands were clasped in his lap. His head nodded forward. As soon as the cruiser began to follow the curves of Neck Road, Clarence Bollinger slept deeply.

Ellery Queen's Mystery Magazine, 1995

The Queen's Angel

She walked over to the gentleman sitting on a weathered bench on Prince Island, an ancient suburb on the south side of the river—part of the city of Amsterdam, Holland's capital. The lady in red sat down next to the little old gentleman.

She said, "You're a nice man, sir."

"I am?" Amsterdam's Chief of Detectives asked.

A cold finger touched his hand. "Yes."

He had been watching a pair of mallard ducks courting on the Waterway ahead. They'd been circling each other, the female in charge and bobbing about; now they were nodding and bowing. He wondered whether he was expected to nod and bow, too.

He thought she was attractive: long-legged, firm-bodied, the red dress demurely expensive. The face might be operated on and she might be in her forties. Her scanty makeup was effective, outlining large, alluring, gleaming eyes, full moist lips, high cheekbones. She had elf's ears, small and pointed, set off against short black hair. She was slim.

"You're neat," she said.

He was. His shantung-cotton suit, somewhat worn, was tailored to fit a slight body elegantly. The new straw hat shaded intelligent pale-blue eyes. He had a straight nose under large gold-framed glasses. His narrow hands rested on the gold knob of a thin bamboo cane.

"Make your point, dear," the Chief of Detectives said firmly.

"You think I'm a whore?." The lady asked.

"Are you?" he asked.

She shook her head. "You think I'm panhandling? For drug money maybe?"

He checked her pupils. "I don't think so, dear."

"Am I bothering you?" the lady in red asked. "I can go away."

An overcultured voice, the Chief of Detectives thought. A university accent? Her manner reminded him of female relatives who had studied at the exclusive University of Leyden. And she seemed self-assured. A successful professional? A lawyer? No, he dealt with lawyers all the time. Lady lawyers are sharp-snooted. She seemed quiet and introverted in spite of her momentarily forward manner.

"M.D.?" he asked.

She laughed. "Correct."

He noticed a diamond ring, a gold watch, the smartly cut red dress again—matching shoes, scarf, pocketbook. The getup seemed suggestive of professionally beautiful models as shown in the magazines his wife kept scattered on coffee tables. "You practice medicine?" he asked.

"Not for some years now," the lady said.

He noted the consistently coldly defensive voice contrasting with her direct pushy manner. His manner of observation was the police manner, of course—always focused on contradictions. The punk in the Rolls Royce, the quietly well dressed gent staggering about drunk in the worst alley in town, the shy pushy lady. The punk stole the car. The gent is about to shoot a male prostitute for blackmail. What did the shy, pushy lady do?

He got up, lifted his hat, said his name, that he was pleased to meet her, put out his hand.

"Marion," she said, shaking his hand.

He sat next to her again. "Marion who?"

"Can I be a little anonymous for now?" Marion asked. "Would you mind, commissaris? Until I know you a little better?"

She would have seen his face in the papers, he thought. He'd been in the news again: a tricky case, he hadn't even solved it. Sergeant de Gier did the work but the journalists liked to have the commissaris' picture in the paper—the wise old man, as the morning paper had it.

"What can I do for you, Dr. Marion?" he heard himself say kindly. Does a wise old man allow his meditations on the weathered bench on Prince Island to be disturbed? He liked to come here to ruminate on the relativity of things. Stare at the rippling river. "Reflections on the sea of illusion." He had read that somewhere.

It was true—the older he got, the less things seemed real.

"I need to ask you something," the lady said.

The guru syndrome, the commissaris thought. The lady wanted free information from above. Why come to me? He thought. What did she think he knew? He was just another ignoramus, bumping about on the miracle, manipulating the riddles, but tell that morning paper. Wise old man.

"I live with death," Marion said.

We all do the commissaris thought, but he didn't say that.

"Everything I live with dies," Marion was saying.

He noticed her voice was hoarsely dead itself, as if a dry wind blew through a delicate mask—her face. The fingers that touched his wrist were cold. Her smile was cold.

He shivered. She withdrew her hand: "Low body temperature commissaris, it's been with me ever since. I'm used to it now."

He saw that her tight skin wasn't due to a face lift. Marion was a live skull. The eyes seemed no longer mysteriously attractive but hollow, quite empty.

"I'm sorry," she said when he shivered again.

"What died?" he asked. "What did you live with that died?"

The process started slowly, she explained. First her house started dying. She always liked growing greenery. She cultivated mini palms and large ferns in a solarium on the back porch. Prize geraniums in the windows. Then all the plants died on her.

"Disease?" the commissaris asked.

Yes, Marion explained, but plant disease can be treated. She washed the palms, dusted the ferns, cut the geraniums down. They withered anyway.

Peabody died, too. Peabody was the dog, a cute little mutt. He got a cancer.

"Was he old?"

"Only five."

Albertine, the Siamese cat, was next.

Marion got a puppy and a kitten from the pound—an undefined virus interfered, they never grew up. She took up horse riding in Amsterdam Forest. Any horse she rode sickened. The stable canceled her membership card. She bought her own horse. Kaiser died, too.

"Of what?"

"Of a shot in the head. His leg was broken."

The commissaris sat quietly.

"Bad luck?" Marion asked.

He told her that that interpretation was her own. He told her about his wife's uncle and the bombing of Rotterdam during World War II. German three-engine Junker airplanes bombed the open city when it refused to surrender to SS commandos smuggled in on river barges. When Dutch marines pushed the enemy back, the Junkers set the city on fire.

Uncle drove to town to try to save expensive merchandise in his store. The warehouse burned. While Uncle watched his uninsured fortune blaze, fleeing folks stole his car. Uncle walked home, and found it flattened—no wife left, no kids. Uncle had always been irritated by breaking shoelaces. At that moment, one broke. Uncle laughed, laughed, laughed.

"The broken shoelace was good luck?" Marion asked.

The commissaris couldn't define the event, but Uncle, having nothing more to lose, became a much decorated freedom fighter. He married again, started a business again, never cared much again.

"Free forever?" Marion asked.

The commissaris pursed thin lips. "Mustn't exaggerate, my dear."

"My story is different, perhaps." Icy lips touched the commissaris' cheek, and he was alone again, watching ducks.

"This isn't over yet," his wife said when he told her that evening, feeling guilty a bit while touching feet under the eiderdown—an intimacy he enjoyed.

"You want to see the lady in red again?" his wife asked.

"Not really, Katrien."

"Then stay away from Prince Island."

The commissaris did that, to please Katrien. He didn't think that age sixty-four, crippled on bad days by a rheumatic hip condition plastic-toothed, coughing painfully at times—he no longer smoked but carbonized lung tissue takes a while to grow back—he presented much of a challenge.

He still wanted, on days off, to reflect on the sea of illusion, so he rented a dory on the Amstel River.

Marion showed up on the dock.

"Mind if I join you?"

"Be my guest."

She had elegant legs. The short red skirt wasn't designed for boating.

"You should play a guitar," Marion said.

"I could sing."

The commissaris sang "My Funny Valentine."

"The Chet Baker version," Marion said. "I used to have the record but it got scratched at parties." She caressed his knee. "You're very courageous, aren't you? I thought that long note had to break until you folded it round." She smiled. "Just barely, but that's all it needs."

"Miles Davis sometimes plays like that," he said.

She smiled. "You must really know jazz."

"Two of my associates play the genre. Adjutant Grijpstra on drums and Sergeant de Gier on flute. They encourage me to join them." He looked at wavelets, set up by a fresh breeze.

"You've been singing long?"

"I sang as a boy," the commissaris said. "Then, for a hundred years, I was too shy. I'm glad my associates got me into it again." He was rowing with long strokes, feeling vigorous for a change. "Jazz singing can reach far."

"How far?"

"All the way?" he asked.

She laughed.

He rowed the dory into a cove. The sun was still warm. Pinstriped carps did their ritual mating dance between waving cattails. A marsh heron, its squat brown-and-yellow body hidden perfectly in shadows of waving reed rushes, startled them by bursting out in booming warning calls like sudden drumbeats.

"Grijpstra sometimes explodes like that," the commissaris said, "and then he's back on the edge of his snaredrum, doing dry ticking: the crackle of understatement that drives the listener wild." He grinned. "It's the understatement that makes jazz truthful."

He had brought a thermos filled with strong coffee and a bag of ginger cookies. She shared his silver mug.

He began to feel cold and blamed his old bones.

"Dear old bones." Marion smiled. "Maybe we shouldn't be meeting like this. Next time we'll have lunch." She told him about a divorced father she hardly knew but ran into in Paris. He had asked her to lunch and they ate fried sole in a little restaurant with a view of the Seine. "The only time we were close."

"I'm a father figure to you?"

"What else?" She laughed her chilly laugh again. "But you're not my father."

"I'd like fatherly advice," Marion said when the dory entered the rental marina.

"All an old man is good for," the commissaris joked.

She didn't pick that up. He noticed again that her mask didn't move. "Even the weeds in my garden are dying," she said. "Do you think it's something I did?"

"What did you do?" the commissaris asked.

She waited until the dory was tied to the dock and he helped her out. "You know I'm a doctor," Marion said, hand on his shoulder, stepping up on the dock. "Doctors heal. But I killed my husband."

The breeze blew his boater into the Amstel. By the time he retrieved the hat, Marion's car drove off.

"A wrong diagnosis, perhaps," the commissaris told his wife. "Doctors can't help making tragic mistakes sometimes. Remember Cousin Jasper?"

"Jasper," Katrien said, "was an apprentice, and the professor in charge was unwell when they brought in the little girl."

"The little girl died," the commissaris said, "because of Jasper's tragic mistake."

"Jasper lives in the country now," Katrien said, "growing tomatoes as a hobby. He also keeps healthy goats. You stay away from that killing woman."

"But, Katrien . . ."

The commissaris and Marion ate fried sole in a restaurant next the Concertgebouw, at his invitation by phone. "How did you locate me?" Marion asked.

He didn't tell her, but it was simple enough. Sergeant de Gier found her. The leads were few but clear: a forty-plus lady called Marion with a Leyden medical degree driving a red Ferrari.

"How did you find me renting the dory?" the commissaris asked. Chance. She happened to see him there. The meeting at Prince Island was chance, too. She knew what he looked like from published photographs and approached him by instinct. "Would you have contacted me again?" he asked.

She said yes, even the huge tree in front of her house had died. "Am I killing the city?"

The sole *a la meuniere*, served whole, larger than the large silver dish it came on, was just excellent, crisp on the bone, tender inside. The little potatoes were good and crumbly. The Belgian endive salad was fresh and chewy. Marion wore a red dress again, not the same as the second time, not the same as the first time. She looked very good in red.

"So you killed your husband?" he asked conversationally. "How'd you do that?"

"I aggravated a psychosomatic condition," Marion said. "Paul thought his heart was bad. His worrying brought on palpitations. I prescribed drugs that made the palpitations kill him."

"Why did you want him dead?"

"I wanted his money," she said, "and I wanted his brilliant friend Bad Bart."

"Define 'bad,'" the commissaris said.

"Do you," Marion asked, "believe that nothing matters?"

"Did Bart?"

"Do *you*?" she asked coldly.

"I believe the experiment of creation is unplanned," the commissaries said, "but I find random evolution fascinating, anyway, perhaps because of its chaotic essence."

She sighed. "Bart talked like that. He found everything senselessly fascinating, including me. I thought I agreed. I wanted to prove my insight, to astonish him. We were reading Sartre then. Bart told me we were free."

"You *are* free," the commissaries said.

"I wish I wasn't," Marion said.

"And nothing matters," the commissaris said. "But maybe there's more to that." He poked about in his sole. "Was it Bart's idea that you would kill your rich husband?"

"No," she said. "He said he couldn't, because of some conditioned hang-up, sleep with a friends wife, so I removed his friend." She massaged her tight cheeks. "Doesn't that sound stupid now?"

"This is like the meeting with your father in Paris?" the commissaris asked.

"No." She put down her fork. "I didn't want anything from him then. We just happened to meet and then we had that nice lunch."

"What do you want from me?" the commissaris asked.

"I want things to stop dying around me." Her voice had become brittle.

"When did this murder happen?"

"It *happened*," she said, "that's my point. Everything happens. We happen. Nothing is planned. Life happened to start up four billion years ago and eventually we happened along with it, and I happened to kill Paul. That's what I thought then—I don't know what I think now."

He had wanted to order the peche melba or a chocolate mousse perhaps, delicacies that replaced nicotine—this was the day he could grant himself a dessert. She wanted only coffee. He sipped his own, watching her smoke.

"You smoke a lot?"

"Rarely." She laughed. "I don't have bad habits. I just killed my husband." She rummaged in her bag and brought out an enlarged snapshot. It showed a smiling male corpse, lying on an oriental rug. It wore a tuxedo. The dead right hand held a note. Penciled handwriting said, "Farewell my love," signed by a red print of lips. A female foot in a red high-heeled shoe rested on the corpse's chest. A long leg. The hem of a red skirt.

"Ah," the commissaris said. "Paul? After the heart attack? He looks pleasant enough to me "

"Boring," she said. "Repetitive. Paul drank a lot."

"*Your* leg?"

"Yes," she said.

"Your note, your handwriting, lipstick imprint of your mouth?"

"Yes, yes," she said impatiently. "Yes!"

"Who took the photograph?"

"I had my camera set up for delay," she said, "with the button on automatic."

"I'm a policeman," the commissaris said. "You sought me out twice. Deliberately. You made an effort. You've managed to make me curious. I may be after you now. You know what you're doing?"

"You think I'm giving myself up? The photograph is proof."

"When did this happen?" the commissaris asked.

She smiled sadly. "Fifteen years ago. Deadline for arrest is after sixteen years. You can still arrest me. I took that photograph to impress bad Bart. It aggravates my crime. Isn't this a good case?"

He played with his napkin. "You've done some research—but have you considered what you're presenting here? A weird confession hardly supported by circumstantial evidence. There was no autopsy?"

She shook her head. "I called in a colleague. She diagnosed heart trouble. A natural death."

"Any witnesses?" the commissaris asked, holding up the snapshot. "Bad Bart saw this happen?"

"No."

"You and Paul were going out?" the commissaris asked.

"To a concert."

The commissaris looked thoughtful. "Oh, dear."

"The evidence might be good," she said. "My handwriting, my leg—"

"No," the commissaris said. "I wouldn't handle the case." He gave her the photo. "The prosecutor wouldn't, either. Neither would a judge. That photo might be a joke, made long before your husband's death, as your lawyer would point out. Your confession could be hysterical." He waved his napkin. "This country's roots are Calvinistic, we're all obsessed with guilt."

"I am now," she said. "I was then. Bart wasn't even bad."

"What happened to the man?"

"Weak Bart didn't like everything dying around me, either, and then he died, too, due to a heroin addiction. He fell off a streetcar."

"You didn't arrange that?"

"No." The cold smile was back. "I was paying for treatment. He slipped out of the clinic."

The commissaris helped Marion into her coat.

"I know what I'm doing," she said while he walked her to the Ferrari. "You're a top-ranking policeman, serving both the citizens and the Queen. The Queen is the crown. The crown is the magic intermediary through which citizens reach divinity. The symbolism is clear. If I apply for grace, I have to see the Queen's angel . . ."

On Sunday morning, the commissaris walked to Marion's house. His hips were hurting again, he couldn't sleep. It was five A.M. The birds were singing, the summer sun filtered pale-orange light through narrow streets. Marion Janssen, M.D., lived, Sergeant de Gier reported, in a silver-grey slender-gable house at Gentlemen's Canal—a most superior address in the old city's very core. She was a widow. Paul Janssen was heir to a brand of good cookies. His death made her rich. And crazed, perhaps, the commissaris thought.

The commissaris was sorry now that something like this had happened to him again. He should have refused. Why would he accept a crazed citizen's bother?

Was he like the German university professor who striptease artist Marlene Dietrich made a despicable fool of in the movie *Blue Angel* that he owned on video—a self-destructive drama he watched sometimes, sipping hot cocoa, when Katrien was out?

Had he wished for a witch?

Was he caught up in some nonsense again?

Then, on the empty quay, in the thin early-summer-Sunday morning's glow, as the only citizen about in a still-dehumanized city, he saw the dead tree.

There were lots of trees on the Gentlemen's Canal, spaced evenly—majestic elms branching out widely, each loaded with a million leaves—but only Marion's tree was dead. Its imposing skeleton gestured bleakly in front of an ailing house. The commissaris checked cracked basement windowsills and doors, painted recently, the paint already flaking off. The massive brass doorknob was dull. The granite steps were cracked. The house, seven stories high, seemed to be leaning far forward. He painfully climbed the steps to the front door, leaning on his cane, peering into the first story windows.

No plants anywhere. No dog yapping. No slinky cat movements. No twittering sparrows, not even a crow in the dead tree, no pigeons fluttering around tiles or gutters. But this is Amsterdam, the commissaris thought, bird city. He did see waterfowl farther up and down the canal. On the water nearby there was only a duck, upside down.

The door opened. Marion, in a red kimono, attempted a smile of welcome. "See the dead duck? You think I shot it because I felt you were coming?"

So he believed her now.

"Explain it to me," Marion said, serving instant coffee.

He shrugged.

She pointed at his chest. "No, you're a chief of detectives, you hold a law degree. The papers say you're a genius. You're a public servant. Am I not the public?"

She slid out of her chair, knelt on the bare floor, touched his foot. "I know I'm doing this to myself. I'm sorry I killed Paul. There is no end to this misery. Please save me."

He just sat there, drinking the instant coffee that he didn't like. A neat little old gentleman who couldn't sleep and went for a walk and landed up in a demon's lair, a dying house in the midst of Old Amsterdam's splendor of graceful Golden Age architecture and ever-alive waterways. He saw the dead duck outside, orange webbed feet upward, mini-sails that caught the wind. He grimaced. The coffee was awful. Why didn't she serve filtered Sumatra, store-roasted at one of the city's deli-outlets? She drove a Ferrari.

"How's the Ferrari, Marion?"

"Carburetor trouble," she said, still kneeling. "The fuel injection gets clogged, too. They keep fixing it wrong. I'm walking everywhere now." She tugged the seam of his crisply ironed trouser leg. "My machines sicken, too."

He almost smiled. The coffee was bad, but having this exotic creature humiliating herself was pleasurable in a way. He sighed. One demon creates another?

"Please," Marion said.

"I'll see what my wife says," he said. "Let me go now and I'll ask her."

"So simple," Katrien said. "Look, I don't like your new woman, but surely she has suffered enough. Just do as I said."

"But Katrien—"

"Just do it."

So the black Cadillac, the Mayor's car—but the Mayor was a friend—drove up, escorted by two white BMW twin-cylinder motorcycles, ridden by extra-tall extra-wide Military Police sergeants—the MP colonel was another friend. The Mayor's driver wore his lackey uniform, with a triangle papier-mâché hat. The sergeants rode in bearskins, white-leather crossbelts and pistol holders, black-baize uniforms, silver buttons, white braid. The commissaris wore similar tunic and tight pants, but his buttons and braid were gold. His hat was flat, with more braid on the visor. Crowns shone on his shoulders. His boots were spit-polish. He wore his short sword.

("Oh, dear—" Katrien had laughed when she dressed him "—oh, dear.")

Marion opened the door. The commissaris, flanked by the sergeants, limped up the stone steps. The sergeants stopped at attention, the commissaris limped on.

Her large sitting room contained nothing but two straight chairs and a small rug. She sat on one chair, he on the other.

"Marion Janssen," the commissaris said, "you sinned, by your own rules, against another lifeform of your species. Since then you have punished yourself. You cannot undo your crime and neither can the crown, but the crown now forgives you. Kneel down on that rug."

He got up and unsheathed his sword. He touched her shoulder with the shiny steel. He sheathed the weapon, stood up straight made his voice sing: "Rejoice and do better!"

"Did she feel better?" Katrien asked when she helped him take the stiff uniform off.

"She did," he said.

She yanked his boot. "Did she kiss you passionately afterward?"

"Please, Katrien," he said, rubbing a painful hip. "She cried, she trembled, she was awed. The poor thing wouldn't dare. I was the Queen's angel."

"Sure," Katrien said.

"But I do believe that horseplay you came up with broke the spell. She says she's off to Florida, to work in a clinic that breeds healthy offspring from damaged waterfowl—pelicans mostly, an endangered species."

"Good!" Katrien kissed his bald spot. "Good. I'm glad."

Ellery Queen's Mystery Magazine, 1991

Happy Hermits

Maybe I wouldn't have made Mister Calahan fall out of his canoe by banging my Tibetan cymbals and yelling Apache curses if it hadn't been Christmas. Christmas always irritates me. For one thing, my parents forgot to have me baptized, and for another, I don't care for loud festivities. I'm retired, I'll have you know. At the eve of life I'm claiming some rest and I've gone a long way to get it, right to the end of the Florida Keys, that graceful line of bridge-connected islands where palm trees sway and pelicans glide. I found myself this pirate's mansion on the shore of Egret Cove and live quietly with a large scraggly bird. Parrot feasts on nuts from the garden and I feast on seafood from the cove —snappers, groupers, broiled or boiled. For exercise I play polite basketball with Deputy Sheriff Wekko, another contented recluse of Egret Key. Wekko still has to work; he drives a patrol cruiser up and down the one and only highway here, U.S. 1. He makes up for dealing with bad humans by feeding friendly raccoons cat food. The raccoons live under his cabin-on-stilts on the other side of this small island. We have our differences; Wekko follows the path of voodoo and I'm more into Tantric spells, but all of us here on Egret Key are just one little bunch of happy hermits.

So where is the catch?

Don Pussiliano is the catch.

The don is a recluse too, after having been a Manhattan banker. He reluctantly admits to maybe having slipped a little—inside trading in *really* junky junk bonds but after playing some good tennis in jail, the don cleared the gate with the remnants of a billion. Then what does Pussiliano do, this foreign-sports-car driver in flashy clothes under a fluffed and glazed hairdo, this complicated incarnate spirit suffering from assorted personality disorders? Of all the places in our vast country, once-almost-a-billionaire Pussiliano has to find Egret Key, buy up all remaining shorelands, and build himself a two-acre palace a stone's throw from Wekko's and my humble abodes.

What the don calls his "cottage" (and Wekko and I call "Donsville") is poured out of concrete and then plastered over to give it the fashionable "Baleares" look: rustic, each window artistically out of line in pastel-colored walls. So far so nice. Now cover this Mediterranean cuteness with a sloped Himalayan-style" roof of multicolored tiles and now what are we looking at? Pizza on a turd? Well, yes, maybe Donsville did get to look like pizza-on-poop, so to distract a neighbor's critical eye Pussiliano throws in a brick terrace to support an African-style beach cabin: round with a straw conical top, like a teenage haircut. Is Donsville looking any better now? Something missing maybe? Well, yes. As Pussiliano keeps hiring and firing architects, a designer with a Transylvanian accent and a Minsk (Czechoslovakia) university degree adds a "Dracula tower": marble-covered, goldtipped, phallic.

Even Wekko, who likes towers, he lives in one himself, was appalled at what the Minsk Vampire Man created.

To finish things off, a redneck crew with chain saws cut down a fine grove of Australian pines that grew between Donsville and my house. From then onward I was exposed to Pussiliano's garish nightmare come true.

Okay, it's a free world. I can look the other way. Can I listen the other way too? When the Makaha Sons of Ni'ihau keep singing *He Ino No Kaiulani* for a couple of hours on end? As a musical backdrop behind call girls entertaining Don Pussiliano on the African-style beach terrace that, since the clear-cutting of my pine grove, I have a technicolor view of?

Listen, I love the Hawaiian Sons, but the don likes to put his Yamaguchi sound system on repeat, and the best music goes bad when the same disc keeps spinning.

The same goes for the best of nearby Key West's pick of young naked women. Will the beauties never drive their Mazda Miatas home to their escort club on Flagler Boulevard?

You don't have to ogle naked women, you say.

Yeah. Sure.

What, my highborn reader, do you think Buddha was doing under the Bodhi tree?

And do you think he liked it?

Maybe the don's interference with Wekko's and my peace of mind is a character exercise thought up by an unemployed god who has a problem with happy hermits.

How far can a god-tested hermit's head bow?

The god tried that out at Christmas.

I thought I had endured all when the holy season came around and Don Pussiliano began to explore his spiritual overdrive. The frenzy that his vast resources allow him to indulge in must be an attempt to relive carefree early days. Christmas, the don told me tearfully after knocking back more of the finest imported cognac—this was during the days we were still on speaking terms—remakes him into the happy toddler he was in the dreamtime in Little Italy, New York. Christmas lights and music bring back the memory of being hugged by voluptuous aunts.

Pussiliano certainly did his utmost to try and recreate those mammal moments.

Once-almost-a-billionaire desires to recreate a dream. America's efficient mail-order network delivers props promptly.

Christmas, all heaven to Don Pussiliano.

All hell to happy hermits Wekko and Jannie.

Never despair.

"You really think this is designed to get us beyond good and evil?" Wekko asked.

I told him the god planned it to improve Relaxed Attitude.

Sure.

Hermit theory reads easy; hermit practice hurts and makes us yell.

There is always the difference. Pussiliano dreamed of big breasted Christmas aunts. Wekko nightmared of having to sing songs without rhythm in a religious home for leftover kids. As for me, a decorated pine tree reminds me of getting whacked over the head with squeaky radio songs, trying to play with malfunctioning toys, of cheek-squeezing Saint Nicks, of banishment to a rat-infested basement for inadvertently setting the *Tannenbaum* on fire.

My horrors returned when I watched my neighbor build his theme park. I shuddered when I saw Pussiliano decorate palm trees, Norway pines? Sea grape trees, even giant cactuses with gaudy colored-lights that switch on and off at random.; I flinched when floodlights showed a stable filled with plastic folks, a placid donkey and bull, cheered by shepherds and bleated at by sheep, all, even the animals, true-size and frozen in exaggerated postures. Don Pussiliano even added the three magi on camels, who raced a fat, uniformed Master HoHoHo whipping reindeer that pulled a sleigh stacked with colored boxes. Plastic Christmas trees lined Don Pussiliano's floating dock, their flashing lights bobbing with the motion of the cove's waves.

So I was going to look the other way, but we were on the waterside here and Egret Cove acts like a mirror. The spectacle reflects for some considerable distance.

A blindfold?

Move about my property by ear?

What about sound pollution?

Pussiliano replayed his one and only seasonal record: *Crescent City* by Wynton Marsalis. Strategically placed stereo speakers piped "Jingle Bells" from everywhere, a little loud but pure and pervasive.

Pure pervasive "Jingle Bells" forever.

Holy jazz on repeat. Here the high-quality compact disc comes round again. "Silent Night." SILENT NIGHT!

Earplugs?

I tried wads of cotton wool but it's hard to move about blindfolded and deaf-plugged. I tried to stay in bed but body needs kept me up and about, in spite of Mr. Marsalis's persuasive version of "God Rest ye Merry, Gentlemen."

Marcus Roberts on piano. A fine and sensitive player indeed. When I heard "Winter Wonderland" the first twenty times, I was quietly moved. From then on I bit my lips so as not to cry loudly.

So when Pussiliano has his Christmas works going—from sunset to the early hours is the usual schedule—I tend to become a wee bit cranky, as I was when Parrot thought he spotted a lobster robber early on the evening of December the twenty-third.

Egret Cove is a nature reserve, and I volunteered to be the sanctuary's keeper. I like doing good work to make up for a bad past.

Hear my confession: Yes, I used to, up in New England, convert wetlands into pricy house lots and make a bundle.

Spoil the North, save the South.

Here I am, feeding disabled pelicans. After boating about the bay taking care of the winged ones, I socialize with my fellow hermit. Deputy Sheriff Wekko is a black skinhead who lives in a pagoda that I helped him build from driftwood. Wekko's wife hated it; she left for the pleasures of Miami. My wife chose the pleasures of heaven; she left me Parrot, a large and scraggly bird. My deceased wife's deceased dog, large, loving, and loud, is still with me in voice, for Parrot, when alarmed, imitates Fido's barking. Parrot likes to ride my shoulder.

"WHAF WHAF!" Parrot barked into my ear.

Now what? We already have "Hark! The Herald Angels Sing" on the super-stereos next-door, and now the loudest Floridian dog ever lives again on my shoulder?

I rushed into the house and grabbed my cymbals.

My house once belonged to a British pirate operating out of the nearby Bahamas. The Royal Navy kept chasing him, so Captain Death moved to American shores. He brought his house with him, having his crew break the structure up and reassembling it after the voyage. Captain Death's sailors were talented artists.

One of their works of art is a board railing that lines the west side of my second floor. A design of silhouettes was jig-sawn into the boards, showing alternate unclad feminine shapes and fat stone jugs. The house is placed in such a way that the setting sun projects the rail design onto my bedroom's whitewashed walls. The slowly moving figures appear as shapely nude women pursuing alcoholic joys. Now that I portend to be a meditating and chanting enlightenment-bent hermit, I should have taken that heathen railing down, especially since it had weathered away a good deal, but I had Wekko help me restore the decoration instead.

I like to test myself.

We must respect the past. This house is a monument. This type of gingerbread artwork from the Victorian era is now exceedingly rare. A good hermit should not shy away from temptation.

There were other rationalizations that slip my mind for the moment.

Captain Death's minions also built him stone seaways and steps. Wekko and I feed the cove's wildlife from there. Seagulls and pelicans glide, fish jump, and lobsters crawl as we throw them leftover dinner. The stone steps, hollowed out from underneath by ever-recurring currents, are home to giant lobsters. Florida lobsters are rare now and consequently pricy. I guard a fortune's worth of fresh lobster tail here. Bad-ass poachers pass my shore in their dinghies and dories. I hear them salivate when they see my tasty crustaceans wave yard-long antennas.

Parrot keeps watch. As soon as his birdly radar notices an evil presence, he barks in my ear and I grab my genuine sorcery cymbals from the pre-Buddhist Bon monastery of Shing Lap Ch'a (I collect bizarre objects) and crash those big copper mothers together. Parrot, propelled up by the cymbals' thunderous clang, loses feathers while shrieking.

I shriek too. For lobster robbers I like to use Apache incantations. Apaches lived by raiding and invented special curses that would paralyze their opponents. I had an Apache girlfriend once. She was a good teacher.

The sudden cacophony is guaranteed to chase away lobster robbers.

Usually I first check who is boating near the stone steps, but with Pussiliano's Christmas Musical going on my patience was short.

CRASH, shriek, ziiiiiingngngngng!

I expected the sound of swishing oars or of an outboard engine starting up but heard the splash of a body hitting water. There were shouts for help. I also heard gurgling and thrashing.

Since when do lobster robbers fall out of boats? Since when can lobster robbers not swim?

I remembered the current.

Now what had I done?

Was I endangering a Keys-supporting tourist?

Egret Cove connects with the Caribbean Sea through just one narrow channel between mangrove swamps. An immense body of water has to rush in and out twice each day, pushed and pulled by the tides. The current swishes by my dock with considerable power. Right then the tidal stream was outward, directed toward the dreaded empire of Cuba. If my victim couldn't swim, his next port of call might be Havana.

Parrot and I rushed to the dock. An expensive canoe was floating away rapidly from growing concentric circles that marked the spot where its owner went under.

I keep a small motorboat at my dock. Fortunately she started right up. Victim hadn't floated off too far; I saw his bubbles and grabbed him with the boat hook.

He responded nicely to life-restoring techniques.

I chased and caught the canoe too.

Back again on my dock, I stripped Victim of his bright yellow silk shorts and orange embroidered cowboy shirt. I wrapped him up in towels. He staggered into the house.

"Are you okay now, sir?"

Victim turned out to be a small middle-aged white male with a nose that got broken and fixed a few times. What hair he had was long. Rolex watch plus solid gold bangles.

I got him a beer while he waited for clothes to come out of the dryer. He said he liked the pirate's mansion. I asked what he might have been doing in his expensive canoe in the dark in a dangerous channel.

Victim identified himself as Mr. Calahan, a birdwatcher from Chicago. He had been studying a large flock of iridescent ibises settling down for the night on the islets farther along the cove. It suddenly got dark (as it will in the tropics). He got lost. He was steering for my stone steps, looking for help, when I clashed my cymbals and shouted my curses. He fell oust of the boat. He was glad I saved him. He wasn't glad that he had lost his waterproof bag with expensive contents.

"Have you seen my bag, my man?"

"So, Sir."

The moon had come up. Mr. Calahan pointed at a pelican with one wing, paddling itself along to his islet. The invalid pelicans of Egret Cove Sanctuary sometimes forget they can't fly so they're often late coming back to the little mangrove islands farther along in the cove.

"*Will* you look at that iridescent ibis, my man?"

I nodded politely. We do have some pretty birds here.

"Iridescent ibises are so rare," Mr. Calahan said. I heard there were still some left on this cove so I came out to look. Watching near-extinct birds makes me happy."

He told me about the islets where he had seen dozens of these nearly extinct birds.

Never, in my fifteen years on Egret Island, did I see an iridescent ibis here.

It's rude to argue with guests.

"Ibises, my man." Mr. Calahan sighed happily.

Well, what is it to me? Just the other day, in Key West, a tourist called my attention to wheeling turkey vultures, calling them herons.

"You must be the caretaker here, my man," Mr. Calahan said.

I said I certainly took a lot of care here.

He smiled at what he believed to be a simpleton's joke. "You're a conch, my man?"

Conchs are what people who are born on the Keys proudly call themselves. Conchs are sly. They get tourists to consider them to be simple-minded. Conchs make more money that way.

I said I would like to be a Conch but that I was Dutch-born.

"Worse!" Mr. Calahan laughed. He said he knew all about where the Dutch-born come from. Holland. Right? Holland is, Mr. Calahan told me, where Dutch uncles (who like to fondle little girls) live. Dutch uncles talk double Dutch (ununderstandable gobbledegook). Dutch uncles take guests out on Dutch treats (guests pay their own tabs). The guests who pay their own tabs are known as "going Dutch" (meaning "going stupid").

Being even simpler than a Conch, I laughed heartily at this amusing information, told slowly by Mr. Calahan so that the Dutch wannabe-Conch caretaker might follow its subtle contents.

I couldn't blame Mr. Calahan though. It's the way I look. No more Brooks Brothers suits for me. I wear jeans now. I patch them myself, and I patch the patches. My suspenders are frayed. My faded linen work shirt doesn't get ironed much. I cut my sandals from a car tire found by the roadside. I don't comb my beard and I cut my own hair. Wekko says I look like I slept in the exhaust fumes of a school bus and the cloud stuck to my head. Uncounted Bostonian martini lunches (in the past, in the past) have made my eyes perpetually bloodshot. A diet of broiled snapper with my secret basil-based sauce keeps me-lean, but key lime pie (a pie a day keeps the doctor away) makes my belly jut out.

"Who owns this historical villa?" Mr. Calahan asked.

I said I worked for the well-known eccentric Egret Cove pelicanthropist Jannie Stevens. Jannie collects pelicans that have lost a wing by a poacher's shotgun or a webbed foot by a twisted fishline. The birds may no longer be able to fly or swim, but they can still flap about the mangroves. They still like to breed there. The young of maimed pelicans will be healthy and normal. Feed the invalid parents and restore the birdlife to the Florida Keys.

Wekko, who had heard my cymbals interfere with the jazz ballad "Twas the Night Before Christmas" (Alvin Batiste on clarinet), came by to enquire. I saw him in time, ran out, and stopped
Wekko's rusty bicycle at my gate. Wekko, off-duty that day, was wearing a hermit outfit too: no footwear, bleached and torn bib overalls, a *Hee Haw* hat. I filled him in on recent events.

"Why is he lying?" Weklso asked. "What's in the lost bag?" I agreed with Wekko that we might want to find out. "He thinks I am the caretaker here."

Wekko said he would be the yard man.

Mr. Calahan's clothes were dry. I walked him back to his canoe. Wekko, kneeling-next to my mower, stuck in the tough Kikuyu grass that I had been trying to cut when it was still light, doffed his straw hat.

Wekko, pointing a flashlight, was studying the mower's innards.

"He's my assistant," I told Mr. Calahan.

"Can you swim, my man?" Mr. Calahan asked.

Wekko said he would try anything once.

"Like a water rat," I said.

Mr. Calahan took time to explain the lost bag incident. He blamed me. He was an experienced boater but nobody is prepared when giant copper cymbals clash in the dark while an unseen madman screams.

Wekko slipped into what he calls "superior southern nigger talk." "You'ze just press charges, Mastah Tourist, and we'll have this here Mastah Caretakah's white ass clapped in irons, get Mastah Caretakah pick up trash on U.S. 1 for a year."

That wouldn't be necessary, Mr. Calahan said. Just find him his lost bag and collect five hundred dollars. He was staying at Egret Inn. Some time soon would be fine. That very evening would be better.

I started up my old F-100 Ford pickup truck and loaded both Mr. Calahan and his canoe.

Egret Inn is close-by.

When I came back, Wekko had gotten his powerful underwater flashlight. We put on snorkel gear and dived into the cove. The bag had moved with the current before getting stuck between some coral, half a mile farther along in the channel. Fortunately the bag was Day-Glo orange and reflected our strobing light. Wekko, flapping his long flippers easily through the cove's murky water, retrieved it.

While we checked the bag's contents, Pussiliano played "Sleigh Ride." Todd Williams's beautiful saxophone's phrasing spread widely over the cove. It was the twenty-third of December, the don had been playing the record since the fifth. John Hendricks, one of my all-time favorites, is the singer on that tune. Mr. Hendricks calls the Christmas deer by name, before telling them to "dash away all." I knew the reindeer names too by then. "Dasher and Dancer and Prancer and Vixen. . ."

"I sometimes like 'O Tannenbaum' better," Wekko said. Wekko, whose cabin is about half a mile away from Donsville, can hear the Marsalis record clearly too.

Mr. Calahan's waterproof bag contained a pair of cheap binoculars, a paperback picture book called *Florida's Fabulous Waterbirds*, a professional-looking radiolike gadget with dials and a telescoped antenna, a bag of apples with a "sale" label, a pack of Monarch king-sized filtertips. When I shook the bag out, a New York subway token fell out.

"Wow," Wekko said.

"Wow," I agreed.

We didn't get it all though. We didn't clearly see that the presence of a New York subway token might confirm Mr. Calahan's New York accent. But didn't he say he was from Chicago? He wouldn't be hiding his true identity now?

The bird book would explain Mister Calahan's knowledge of the iridescent ibis, even if he didn't know what a pelican was.

Why buy pie-cover apples when exotic fruit is plentiful on the Keys? Monarch is an unadvertised low-price supermarket type of cigarette, about fifty cents cheaper than a name-brand.

Why would a man who counts his pennies offer five hundred bucks to retrieve fifty-dollar binoculars and an unidentified electronic gadget?

Wekko and I can't have been thinking.

I switched on the yard lights so we could play basketball before dinner, doing long shots—we're both bad at that. Missing shots makes us walk around. When we walk around we talk.

"What do you think that radio thing was?" Weldo asked.

I said it might be a shortwave radio. Tourists who watch iridescent ibises may be interested in what the weather is going to be. Maybe the birds will be covered by clouds. Hard to see them then, right?

Wekko laughed. "But this time of the year the weather never changes."

Yes, sure, but what do tourists know?

Wekko agreed that tourists know nothing. Neither here nor where they come from. Where they come from nobody knows nothing so they can't impress each other much, but when they are here, waving their credit cards, buying weird-looking weather radios and expensive canoes, the Conchs are impressed.

"Wait a minute, Deputy Sheriff Wekko," I said, "how do you know he bought that canoe? Wouldn't he just rent it?"

Wekko knew because none of the local boat-renting shops carried that type of canoe. Whenever rental agencies lose their equipment, the deputy sheriffs race around to find it. Wekko also knew that plastic canoes are sold by the sport store in nearby Key West. One thousand dollars even.

We could have figured that part of the puzzle too, but we didn't.

Why didn't Mr. Calahan rent a rowboat for twenty dollars a day? Why spend a thousand dollars on a plastic canoe?

Because rental agencies only accept credit cards? The credit cards serve as identification. If the boat disappears, the rental agency knows where to find the tourist. But a store has no interest in the identity of a cash client. Mr. Calahan could do his job, let the canoe drift to Cuba. Whatever he got for the job would be a multiple of the cost of the boat and the radio transmitter.

Maybe Wekko and I were puzzled. Maybe we wanted to be puzzled.

Pussiliano was cranking up his sound equipment again.

"Jannie," Wekko shouted, "didn't you say that Pussiliano told you he almost made a billion crooking investors in New York?"

There was too much Christmas racket going on so I didn't answer, but I was thinking about the junky junk bonds. The worst. About Pussiliano selling them. Buying them back cheap when he knew how to make them suddenly go up in value again, confusing clients with "inside" rumors, trading back and forth, to and fro, down and up, long and short, always at great profits.

Another bit of the puzzle that we didn't want to fit in.

Making other people lose big bucks so that he could pick them up would make Pussiliano enemies who could trace him to Egret Key, where he was so visible in the Baleares/Himalayan/Transylvanian/African palace.

Disgruntled and vengeful clients who made propositions Pussiliano couldn't refuse, but maybe had to refuse.

How could the don pay back millions out of the almost-a-billion he maybe owned once? Oh dear oh dear.

I had seen Pussiliano's trash bins standing outside. The bins were stuffed with financial flyers, leaflets, forms, and magazines the investment freak needs for his daily trades. I noticed the computer printouts with fat lines going down, down, down forever. Empty bourbon bottles and beer cans decorated the torn and crumpled paperwork. Pussiliano, former Wall Street whiz kid, was gambling again, this time well away from the huming hub of Manhattan. The don, an outside trader now, was chalking up big losses. I could see that from what the garbage truck picked up each week. He could see it himself while his speakers thundered "Silent Night."

And here was Mr. Calahan canoeing through the silent night, holding a remote control that sets off bombs.

We could have figured it out. Could we have warned Pussiliano?

As Wekko pointed out later, that would have been hard.

Maddened by "Jingle Bells," I had tried phoning the noisy neighbor. Each time his taped voice said it didn't want to be bothered and that no messages could be left after no beep.

I had seen him moping about his terrace that day. Don Pussiliano, in spite of Christmas, had gotten himself depressed. When depressed, he would stay in bed mornings, work out late afternoons, drink evenings. The discipline didn't work. Late sleeping made him gloomier. Lifting weights, although it does enlarge the muscular chest that impresses ladies, gave him a backache. Alcohol made him stick a handgun's barrel into his mouth and play with the gun's trigger.

There had been some changes and shifts in our neighborly relationship. We used to wave, but then my dock got loose one stormy evening and floated against his dock. The banging irritated Pussiliano. Instead of calling me or securing the dock himself, he poured gasoline on the offensive structure and lit a match. Tarred planks burn good. The flames woke me, but he wouldn't let me carry my fire extinguisher over. When I kept coming he fired a shotgun over my head.

There was also the time his Mazeratti sports car, driven by drunk hands, crumpled up my picket fence.

There had been stone throwing at poor old Parrot.

The gods testing a hermit's patience.

"Five hundred dollars," Wekko said. "What say I go to the inn to collect our reward?"

Wekko knew full well the money was no issue. He doesn't care for money himself and I have plenty. The question was asked because I'm the senior happy hermit here, mumbling Tantric Buddhist mantras before sunrise every morning.

Wekko wanted my permission before his next action would restore our peace and quiet.

SILENT NIGHT! boomed the speakers.

Wekko, bag in hand, ready to step on his rusted bicycle, looked at me while Mr. Marsalis led his group into a repeat of "Carol of the Bells." Pussiliano was turning a dial, the beautiful music got louder, changing pleasure into pain. Farther along, on the islets of the pelican sanctuary, nervous baby birds would be tumbling from their nests. Pelican parents do not retrieve their fallen babies.

I sighed.

I thought of the fishbone that nearly choked Wekko when we tried to have dinner with John Hendricks chanting the names of the reindeer. "Dasher and Dancer and Prancer and Vixen . . ."

"I would really like to return that radio gadget to Mr. Calahan now," Wekko said.

I dialed Pussiliano's number.

The rude answering tape was still on.

I looked across the picket fence between Donsville and my property. Just a few days earlier on, crazed by the reindeer's name chanting, I had shouted the don's name. A palace window opened, a Browning automatic shotgun barrel appeared. I ducked as Pussiliano kept pulling the trigger and buckshot kept tearing up the leaves of my banana trees.

Wekko was present at the time but, being a neighbor and therefore personally involved, couldn't follow up himself. He suggested calling in fellow officers. We decided against that. Once-almost-a-billionaire can explain in court why he fired shots to warn off a madman. Pussiliano would also bail himself out pronto and get back to the Christmas carols with a vengeance.

I took full responsibility in the end, like the time a porcupine was eating my quaking aspen, destroying the delicate tree, and Wekko cocked his service revolver and looked at me and I nodded sadly and said, "Sure."

Down went the porcupine.

Down went Don Pussiliano, or every-which-way-at-once rather, the next evening, the twenty-fourth, Christmas Eve.

Wekko, after my fateful "sure," bicycled off, barefoot, in his bib overall, with a straw behind his ear, a simple mower of lawns, on his way to Egret Inn to deliver a bag of what the innocent manual laborer presumed to be lost and found birdwatcher's tools, and collect five hundred big ones from Mr. Calahan, a rich Chicago tourist.

Mr. Calahan grabbed the bag and paid up.

"What's your name, my man?" Mr. Calahan asked.

Wekko doffed the remnants of his hat. "Malcolm XI, Sah."

That was the twenty-third.

December twenty-fourth, minutes after sunset, the body of Don Pussiliano was torn to shreds, to the tune of "God Rest ye Merry, Gentlemen," by flying objects cast from hard plastic. The objects were parts of exploded Christmas sculptures. Heads of Dancer and Prancer, branches of imitation trees, the feet of Father Christmas, the tail of a magi's camel, the body of the Infant tore themselves loose and killed their collector.

The Merry Gentleman rested forever after his huge Sony loudspeakers burned. Later Donsville itself burned too, because flaming Joseph and Mary fragments broke through windows and got stuck in carpets and curtains.

The Fire Brigade, due to tourist Christmas traffic clogging U.S.1, arrived too late to save the building.

The police arrived too.

What could I tell them?

When the plastic puppets killed Pussiliano I was in my room, blindfolded, ears plugged.

Suddenly the ground trembled.

A Christmas earthquake? I removed fold and plugs, ran outside, saw the devastation next door, found a phone, dialed 911.

"You did good," the state police detective said.

"So what happened?" I asked.

"Bunch of computerized bombs placed by a perp who sneaked in by boat," the detective said. "Bombs may have been triggered by the same computer wizard, watching from the cove maybe."

The state police detective said he hated computers and everything computers stood for. Didn't like to deal with computers. If perps were going to kill each other off by hard-to-trace computer, okay, let them do it.

"Well, Officer," I said, "I did see a birdwatcher who didn't know about birds prowling about last night. What if he stuck the bombs in Pussiliano's Christmas ornaments? Suspect said he was staying at Egret Inn."

The detective went to check at the inn. He was back in minutes.

"Looks like we have a hit man here," the detective said. He also said he didn't care for hit men. "Professionals, right? Leave no records. Pay cash. The canoe perp used is still at the inn. Perp didn't rent a car but got himself driven about in cabs. Taxi took him to the airport tonight." The detective pointed in the direction of Miami. Half-hour flight. Up and away." He said he hated perps who flew away in planes.

The detective left. Wekko came in to play a little basketball and to ask what was for dinner.

"Wekko," I said, "I think we should give up hermiting. I think we failed our tests. We didn't have a relaxed attitude. We actually killed a man just because he played a little Christmas music."

Wekko shrugged. "Nah."

"Nah what?"

"We didn't kill Don Pussiliano," Wekko said. "I did, by returning that radio transmitter to the hit man so that he could canoe back to Donsville and blow up the don."

"You asked for my permission," I said.

Wekko thought that was funny. He was a grown-up happy hermit now, he could make his own decisions.

So why ask me, the senior hermit?

Just to be polite, Wekko said. Why worry anyway? If he hadn't returned the bag, the hit man still had time to pick up a new transmitter at Radio Shack in Key West, or the parts to build one. This is America, an efficient, helpful country. Not returning the gadget wouldn't have saved Pussiliano's life.

I felt like a little nitpicking. Why would a hit man who smokes discounted cigarettes pay five hundred hard-earned dollars to retrieve fifty dollars' worth of a replaceable gadget?"

"To remove the evidence, Jannie."

We played basketball, with me missing the basket a lot while I thought. I wasn't quite my former happy self yet. Pussiliano wasn't going to be missed and I planned to have the pelican sanctuary buy the remains of Donsville so that we would never hear bells jingle again, but what about Mr. Calahan? Our returning the gadget had, as Wekko pointed out, removed evidence. The professional killer, a man harmful to society would now be even harder to catch. Shouldn't happy hermits do good? Help to remove bad hit men?

"Nah," Wekko said.

I broiled a freshly caught grouper and served it with my secret herb sauce, but the fish could have tasted bettter.

"You want to improve the world?" Wekko asked. "What sort of a detached hermit are you?"

We had discussed the issue before. Wekko claimed that hermits see through evil, they don't try to remove it.

"But we have a professional killer here, Wekko. Why didn't we catch Mr. Calahan? We had all the evidence, we could have picked up on the pelican-ibis confusion, the New York-Chicago lie, the transmitter-weather-radio mix-up."

"Did we want to?"

"It's never too late, Wekko."

"Aren't you happy Donsville is gone?" Wekko asked.

Yes, of course I was.

"So *be* happy."

In the end Wekko took pity on me. If I didn't want a bad guy, a sadistic killer who puts bombs in Christmas puppets, around, well, so be it.

"Let's do our stuff," Wekko said.

Voodoo stuff scares me. Wekko has some skills, but for a serious exercise like the one we were planning he needed assistance. What happens when a black African nihilist skinhead and a crazed white European pursuer of truth join their death rays? Wekko has his own magic disciplines and I have been into the Tantric exercises for years now, but the idea was to liberate myself, kill off the ego, that sort of ideal stuff; I had never tried my hand at getting rid of bad guys.

I wouldn't let a fellow happy hermit slave by himself though.

Wekko and I can both sew, and we have some artistic talents. We made a doll with yellow pants and orange shirt, gave him a crooked nose and long greasy hair.

"He looks good?"

"He looks good."

We burned bad incense around little Mr. Calahan; I clashed my cymbals, softly this time, and whispered the Apache curses; I danced and concentrated. Wekko, just in case Mr. Calahan had some dark forces of his own, went all out that night. When Wekko chants voodoo my dentures clatter.

The doll, as it was thrown by Wekko into my trash can after the ceremony was over, looked, by the way happenstance made it point its little arms, as if it were diving. "Did you see that?" Wekko asked.

I imitated the doll's involuntary posturing.

Wekko nodded. "So you saw it."

"What does that mean, sorcerer Wekko?"

It meant that Mr. Calahan would be diving too.

And what would the squeaky sounds mean? The terrified mad

chirping coming from the trash can?

"Mice?" Wekko asked.

Yes. Right. But in voodoo?

Wekko said we would soon find out.

I really don't understand voodoo at all, maybe that's why it scares me.

What particularly frightens me now is that voodoo can go back in time. We did our ceremony at eleven P.M. and Mr. Calahan died around ten P.M., we heard that the next day: on Channel 5, the twenty-fifth, Christmas morning.

"An unidentified tourist," our bright and beautiful TV news reader said, "died bizarrely last night off U.S. 1, Milepost 11, on the east side."

Wekko figured it all out later, from police reports at the sheriff's office and from a private investigation he conducted out of Key West.

Mr. Calahan—his real name was Victor Irk Russo, a suspected "hired gun," never charged, never caught—missed his plane because the cab that took him from Egret Key to nearby Key West airport had a flat tire. There was no other plane scheduled out of Key West that night. Eager to get out of the small insular Keys into the vast mainland, Mr. Calahan now needed private transport. As he didn't carry any identification, he couldn't rent a car. Cabs willing to drive the 124 miles to Miami are hard to find on Christmas Eve.

Cars are easily stolen from drunks. Mr. Calahan visited the Red Parrot, a topless bar off Duval Street, Key West. He bought a few rounds, tried to sip soda pop himself, but the girls made him drink alcohol along with the other clients.

We all have our weaknesses. Mr. Calahan was a drinking man. After the tension of the last few days, urged on by attractive companions, our alcoholic succumbed, but he did manage to lift a fellow drunk's car keys. The keys fitted a new Toyota pickup parked behind the Red Parrot.

There's only one road out of Key West. As he drove along a two-lane part of U.S. 1, a cyclist swerved into the Toyota's path.

Mr. Calahan overreacted. The truck drove into the mangrove swamp on the side of the highway.

Mr. Calahan now panicked. He worried that the caretaker and the yardman of the house next-door to Donsville, suspicious after the fire and death, would have passed the "birdwatcher's" description to the police.

Apart from facing a possible murder charge, he was now definitely drunk behind the wheel of a stolen vehicle.

"He dived into the swamp," Wekko said.

So, fine, he would get a little wet, the bugs would bite, eventually someone would see the fugitive flounder about between the air-roots of the mangroves, the cops would pick him up, etc. He wasn't dead yet.

You never know what you get with voodoo.

Giant sea crocodiles are an endangered species and there may be only a few left in our swamps, but Wekko's and my combined spiritual efforts sure as hell raised one.

The pretty news reader showed a picture. The beast was decorated with Christmas garlands, blown out to sea by the Donsville explosions.

According to witnesses on U.S. 1, Mr. Calahan only stopped yelling when the giant crocodile bit off his head.

Ellery Queen's Mystery Magazine, 1995

Non-Interference

"To Dingjum?" Adjutant Grijpstra of the Amsterdam Municipal Police asked. "That's a long way off, Sergeant. That's in the north. You sure?" He looked at Sergeant de Gier suspiciously. De Gier's tall, wide shouldered body sprawled behind his dented desk with his feet propped up on its top, between files not arranged neatly. Sunlight glinted off his pistol's butt and barrel, protruding from a well-worn shoulder holster that contrasted crudely with the sergeant's spotless, tailored blue shirt. De Gier smiled innocently, showing strong white teeth and sparkling, oversized, soft brown eyes. His mustache, model cavalry officer, previous century, was swept up neatly under his long straight nose and high cheekbones supporting a noble brow, supporting thick brown curls in turn.

"Sure," the sergeant said. "I think we should go to Dingjum. It'll be a nice day today, we have just been supplied with a new car, Dingjum is a pleasant little town, set in unspoiled country, we'll drive along Holland's longest and neatest dike, with the sea on one side and a lake on the other, we'll watch birds, sails on the horizon, interesting cloud formations—the car has a sunroof, we can drive and watch the sky in turns—I think I'm sure It's a lovely idea."

Adjutant Grijpstra sighed. His hands, clasped on a steadily rising and receding round belly, covered by a pinstriped blue waistcoat, gently unhooked their fingers and rose in feeble protest. "Dingjum is some sixty miles outside of our territory, Sergeant. We're specialists, members of the celebrated Murder Brigade, we only move for specific and urgent reasons. Whatever could demand our presence in the little rural town of Dingjum?"

Sergeant de Gier withdrew his feet and jumped up in one extended, graceful and lithe, powerful movement. He found a newspaper on a filing cabinet and handed it to the gray-haired solid adjutant, still at ease in his swivel-chair on the other side of the small gray-painted room. "Front page news. Absorb its contents. *Fresh* contents. This happened less than a week ago."

Grijpstra read. He mumbled. "A *Chinese* businessman? In *Dingjum*? An *arrow* into his throat? While watering exotic plants in a *greenhouse*?"

The sergeant poured coffee from a thermos-flask into paper cups. "Exotic is right."

Adjutant Grijpstra put the newspaper down and reached for the coffee. "Thanks. I still fail to see what we could do in Dingjum. There's State Police out there. We would interfere. They might not like that."

"We're never liked," Sergeant de Gier said, contentedly sipping behind his desk again. "However, there might be an exception. Lieutenant Sudema is in charge of the local station; you remember the lieutenant?"

Yes," Grijpstra said. "That was a while ago. I didn't care for all the tomato salad he made us eat."

"And we gave Lieutenant Sudema the credit for our solution," De Gier said gently. "We always do when we can. We're not so bad, Adjutant."

"Oh, but we are," Grijpstra said. "We disturb the peace of our esteemed colleagues. We did that time. The lieutenant didn't exactly welcome us. And we had a legal excuse then; we don't have one now. We found a corpse in Amsterdam that lived, when still alive, in Dingjum. We pursued a hot trail. We're pursuing nothing now."

"I sort of like going after nothing," the sergeant said softly. "Oh, come on now Grijpstra. An arrow in a millionaire's throat and the millionaire is a Chinese who officially resides in the Fiji Islands but who somehow owns a capital villa here, and who originated in Taiwan, and who has married one of our former beauty queens and who owns a factory of computer parts that he doesn't manage; it's all in the article; that's a lot of nothing that adds up nicely."

"Where?" Grijpstra said looking at the paper again. "Ah. The tale continues on page three. Let's see." He turned pages holding the paper up to get a better look at the dead man's wife. "Why does she wear a tiny two-piece bathing suit? Ah, that was her prize-winning outfit. Some years ago. Still a bit of a girl then. Though definitely sexy. A woman now, eh what? A most attractive woman?"

"You bet;" De Gier said. "You'd meet her, if we would go to

Dinjum. Don't you want to meet with a mature beauty queen?"

"Nah," Grijpstra said.

"You do," De Gier said. "And more than I. You've repressed your lusts; there's an evil power in you, pushing its tentacles through your flimsy defenses. You'd go a long way to be able to meet a sex symbol in her dainty flesh. Maybe she shot that arrow? If the Chinese dead man was a millionaire? The couple has no children. Wouldn't the lady make a first class suspect? You could manipulate her, ask her tricky questions, prod her luscious soul, wiggle, finger, feel. . ."

"What's with you?" Grijpstra asked furiously.

"Spring," De Gier whispered. "Spring brings out romantic desire in me. It's a good spring now and we could go for a drive."

Grijpstra pulled himself free of his desk and swiveled his chair. His short legs, in trouserpipes that were rather badly rumpled, and sagging socks and shoes that hadn't been recently polished, scissored slowly. "Yeh," Grijpstra said. "Never mind your romantic needs for now. A Chinese multimillionaire living off the fat of our land, and officially residing in the Fuji Islands, what does that lead to?"

"Non-payment of taxes," De Gier said. "Easy question, easy answer. It also points to extreme cleverness."

The adjutant's heavy body made another complete turn, while a steady sun ray highlighted his short silver hair. "How so?"

"Our corpse," De Gier said, "the former Lee Dzung, married one of this country's certified beautiful women. Why? To kill a whole flock of fat ducks with one broadside of his foreign gun. He doesn't pay taxes in Holland, right?"

"Right," Grijpstra said. "In Fiji, tax would be nominal. But Dzung is active in business here. His factory produces high priced products."

"Now then, Adjutant. Dzung is our guest, he flies in and out, and when he's here he has a beautiful villa, it says so in the article, surrounded by a park, which is owned by his wife, and he owns his wife."

"Yes," Grijpstra said. "If Dzung owned property here he would have to become a resident and pay Dutch income taxes. A diabolic way out that would satisfy human greed, and Dzung picked the best looking wife the country could provide, doubly attractive to him for she is of another race. Long-legged, full-bosomed, golden-haired." Grijpstra studied the photograph again, grunting with pleasure. "A dirty boy's dream. The answer to all his hidden filthy desires."

"You're so Calvinistic," De Gier mused. "Maybe you become over excited when you contemplate that perfect and inviting shape, but why should Dzung?"

"It's natural," Grijpstra said. "Aren't Chinese Confucianists? Confucianism preaches a strict code of morals, an impossible system that automatically produces pleasurable guilt." Grijpstra grinned. "Show me a Chinese beauty queen and my feelings of forbidden lust will be doubled, too. Now suppose I could marry her, and put her in a pagoda, and spend a few months a year with her in a, to me, exotic setting, and have expert foreigners produce my pricy gadgets, and make tax-free profits. . .for that's another point here. . ." —the adjutant's blunt forefinger poked in the direction of De Gier's immaculate shirt—". . .if the Dingum factory is owned by a mother company in far-off Fiji, full profits can be channeled there."

De Gier got up, reaching for a silk scarf of a delicate babyblue color that went well with his indigo shirt. "Shall we go?"

"Whoa," Grijpstra said.

De Gier knotted his scarf, tucking it neatly into his collar.

"An excuse, Sergeant?" Grijpstra pleaded. "We do need an excuse."

De Gier scratched his strong chin. "Yep. Let's see now. About a month ago a bum fell into the Emperor's Canal. The water police fished him out last week. Remember?"

"Yagh." The adjutant grimaced.

"You're telling me," De Gier said. "I almost fainted when they brought that mess in."

Grijpstra looked stern. "You fell into my arms. Was the bum connected to the North?"

"If he wasn't he is now," De Gier said. He opened a drawer and found a disheveled file. "No, right. He *was* from the North. We haven't checked the death properly yet. An accident probably, the man was an alcoholic, but he could have been pushed. He will have relatives in the North and we can check with the register of his place of birth, which is, let's see now, the town of Dokkum."

"Close enough to Dingjum," Gijpstra said. "Then on the way back, remembering all that-tomato salad Lieutenant Sudema made us eat, when we consulted him on that other case..."

"...we sort of casually drop in and ask how the lieutenant has been doing of late."

"Adjutant Grijpstra," Lieutenant Sudema said. "How nice to see you. And Sergeant de Gier. What a pleasant surprise." The lieutenant, splendidly uniformed, saluted his colleagues. He stood between two plane trees, artfully cut so that their branches framed his station, housed in a medieval brick cottage with a pointed gable that carried a stone angel, grasping for a trumpet that had been missing for a century or so. "Amazing. I haven't seen you for a year, a Chinese businessman is most mysteriously murdered here, and you pop up, on a lovely day like this. Out of the blue." The lieutenant pointed at the sky. "It *is* a nice day, today, don't you think?"

"Happened to pass by," Adjutant Grijpstra said. "We were checking the register in Dokkum regarding a dead drunk at our end and..."

"Dokkum is south of here, of course," the lieutenant said. "Close to the highway. But you came up another ten miles just to say hello."

"How's your wife?" De Gier asked.

"You came to see my wife?" Lieutenant Sudema asked. "I see. You're a bachelor, and from Amsterdam, of course; a wicked city, in our provincial eyes that is. Free sex hasn't exactly penetrated here. My wife is well, Sergeant. You did make quite an impression on her the last time you darkened our doorstep. Would you like to meet her again? She's at work now but she'll be back later today. You could wait."

De Gier scratched his right buttock. "You're making him nervous," Grijpstra said. "I've known the sergeant some ten years by now and he's quite shy with women. They'll have to attack him to get anywhere and they'll have to be single."

"My wife isn't single," Lieutenant Sudema said.

"I know;" De Gier said. "I was merely inquiring whether Gyske is in good health."

"You're not interested in my murder?"

"He is," Adjutant Grijpstra said, "and so am I. Any progress?"

The lieutenant asked his guests in and found comfortable chairs. A constable brought coffee. He was sent out again to bring in two bags of large fresh tomatoes from the lieutenant's private crop. Sudema discussed tomatoes for a while, and their diseases. The lieutenant's tomatoes were disease-free but that was only because...

"Right," Grijpstra mumbled from time to time. "You don't say," Sergeant de Gier murmured once in a while.

"So Mr. Lee Dzung was shot dead with an arrow, was he?" Grijpstra asked.

"So we thought," Sudema said.

"He wasn't?" De Gier asked.

"No," Lieutenant Sudema said. "If it had been an arrow, the case might have been hard to crack. There are these newfangled crossbows now, with telescopes; horrible weapons I'll have you know, and all over the place. I thought it had to be one of those. There was an article about crossbows in the Police Gazette that I had happened to read, and some of the weapons make use of small darts. When I saw the corpse; some metal protruded from the wound, sharp and gleaming. So I thought it was a dart. But you know what it really was?"

"Do tell." The sergeant sat forward in his chair.

"A...," the lieutenant opened a drawer in his desk and checked with his notebook, "...what was it called now; right, here, a *shuriken*."

"A what?" Grijpstra asked.

"Metal disc," De Gier said. "Shaped like a star with a hole in the middle. A *shuriken* isn't shot but thrown. A very deadly weapon, Adjutant, when it flies from the hand of a trained assassin."

The lieutenant pushed his chair back. "So, you see, the case is out of my hands. Are you ready for lunch? The local pub still serves its famous lamb chops with the local tomato salad, made out of my tomatoes, of course. I trust you'll be my guests?"

They walked along a country lane, shaded by tall elms. The lieutenant and the sergeant strode along and the adjutant panted, bringing up the rear.

"Why is the case out of your hands?" Grijpstra asked, wheezing between words.

The lieutenant waved airily. "State Security took over. As soon as the pathologist dug up that, what was it now?"

"*Shuriken*?" De Gier asked.

"Right, as soon as we found that a bizarre Far Eastern weapon had been used, we drew our conclusion. Mr. Dzung manufactures a new type of computer chip. That holds more information better, and is capable of programming computers in a most superb way. He makes them in Taiwan. Now he also makes them here. Why? Eh?"

"Why?" De Gier asked.

"You don't know?" Lieutenant Sudema stopped in his tracks. The adjutant bumped into him. De Gier caught them both. "No," De Gier said.

"Is Taiwan close to Russia?" Sudema asked. "Listen, Sergeant, that part wasn't clear to me, either; all I knew was that some outlandish weapon was used, so the killer wasn't Dutch. Mr. Dzung is Chinese. The killer probably, too. Two Chinese visited here last week. I inquired at Mr. Dzung's factory and the manager, a Dr. Haas, tells me that the other Chinese had argued with Mr. Dzung, in Chinese, of course, so he didn't know what about. He assumed that the other Chinese wanted something that Mr. Dzung wouldn't give. An assurance perhaps. That's what the conversation sounded like. Much shouting back and forth."

"Taiwan is friendly with America," Grijpstra said.

Lieutenant Sudema clapped his hands. "Right, you're so right. The State Security chaps, called in by me, working overtime, in the weekend and all, telexed with the CIA. It was all clear at once. Dzung manufactures special computer chips in Taipeh—that's the capital of Taiwan—with American know-how, and with his own, too, for Dzung was a genius and came up with considerable improvements that he
patented at once. Those chips may not be sent to Russia, though it's easier to send stuff to Russia from here than from Taiwan."

"And the two Chinese that came to yell at Dzung?" the sergeant asked.

"Assassins," the lieutenant whispered. "*Ninjas*. Ever heard of them? The most dangerous killers on Earth. They could have killed Dzung straight off but they were good enough to warn him first. Dzung didn't listen. So?" The lieutenant stood on one left, produced a transparent object from his trouser pocket, swung his body from the hip and let go of the object. "*Zip!*"

"Wow," De Gier said, "Ninjas in Dingjum. Throwing a *shuriken*, Tsssshhh!"

"Nah," Grijpstra said.

"You don't believe it?" Lieutenant Sudema asked. "I'm sorry to hear that. I wouldn't believe it at first, either, because, let's face it, Adjutant, we're staunch Dutchmen here, very limited in our outlook and ways. We don't throw exotic razor-sharp steel stars at each other. The very idea. But why wouldn't some nasty outside fellow throw a whatdoyoucallit on Dutch territory? It's a big bad world out there and it does interfere with us at times. We may as well face that."

"You really don't believe in the lieutenant's theory?" De Gier asked Grijpstra. "If a *shuriken* was found in Mr. Dzung's throat, then somebody threw it."

"Not a ninja" Grijpstra said. "Ninja, indeed. Ridiculous. One of these black hooded chaps that slither about on slippers? A ninja in Dingjum would be as conspicuous as a man from Mars."

"I didn't see the Chinese," the lieutenant said. "State Security is making an effort, but they won't catch them; so much is sure. Those ninjas got out of the country immediately after they had fulfilled their contract. Slipped across the border to Germany, flew out of Frankfurt—so State Security presumes."

"Crazy;" Grijpstra said.

Lieutenant Sudema towered over the adjutant and glared down from under the visor of his immaculate cap. "So what else, colleague?"

Grijpstra looked up. "His wife, maybe? Did you interrogate his wife?"

Sudema marched on. De Gier loped along next to him. Grijpstra hobbled behind. The lieutenant turned. "That poor girl had a bad deal; she's better off now. Dzung didn't turn out to be a nice man. Do you know that he wouldn't even let her out of his grounds? He treated her something terrible, like a slave almost. As his sex object; she was just another possession. Everything was in her name. The car. The house, but he kept her short. Wouldn't even pay for driving lessons."

"So the pathetic doll did pretty good out of that murder." De Gier said brightly.

Sudema flapped a hand. "Makes her a suspect, sure. You don't think I didn't see that? Listen, Sergeant. Mr. Dzung got killed at 11:05 AM; a gardener saw him fall. At that moment, Mrs. Dzung was in the basement, operating a laundry machine, being assisted by a maid. She's not good at sports. She was nowhere near."

"I would like to see the location," Grijpstra said. "After lunch of course. I wouldn't miss your tomato salad. Eh, De Gier? Remember that tomato salad? With that delicious dressing? Made with herbs from the lieutenant's lovely wife's very own garden?"

Mrs. Dzung stood in the open doorway. De Gier gaped. Grijpstra stepped back in abject wonder. Mrs. Dzung looked even better than in the photograph they had studied. She was tall, very tall, but perfectly proportioned. She was also well-dressed, in tight leather dark trousers and a flowing white blouse. Her long hair wasn't blond but gold, and as fine as the rays in a spider's web, and luxurious, cascading down her supple shoulders. Her large eyes were sparkling blue and seemed semi-transparent. With the pure color reaching inward, attracting the observer into their unfathomable depths. Her nose was finely chiseled and her lips full, though tight in contour. They parted to smile down at her audience. "Hello Lieutenant."

Sudema introduced his companions. Mrs. Dzung was called Emily, she said in a voice that vibrated pleasantly, soothingly, De Gier thought; there was a motherly quality to the woman though she still had to be quite young, in her early twenties, no more. De Gier felt that he wanted to be lifted up and pressed into those giant breasts, turned up side down like a cat that is cuddled, a large tomcat that will purr and meanwhile reach out with a sly paw, pushing gently, kneading firmly, begging for a kiss from those supple and moist lips.

"Minny to my friends," the vibrating voice murmured.

"I'm your friend," De Gier said. He felt very friendly. He would hold her hand and they would jog along friendly beaches, past a friendly sea, and then run up a dune and be really pally between the wildflowers and the waving grass.

"My colleagues," Lieutenant Sudema said, "would like me to show them around your garden. This must be painful to you, Minny, you don't have to come along."

"Come back for tea," Mrs. Dzung said. "I'll have it ready on the rear terrace." Her eyes met De Gier's, expressing a special invitation. "Yes;" De Gier said, "oh, yes, for sure!"

"She likes you," Sudema said as he took them to the greenhouse. "She likes me, too. We're as tall as she. She told me she doesn't like looking down on men. I'm married."

"Dzung was small-sized?" Grijpstra asked.

"Fat, too." Sudema's face showed some degree of well meant pity. "She told me pudgy men turn her off completely."

De Gier nodded. "Fat men have a hard time. Drag all that weight around while available women turn away. Lonely, heavy. . ."

"Who's fat?" Grijpstra asked. "Tell me, is the factory's director, this Dr. Haas you mentioned, fat? Dzung didn't run his company, right? He couldn't because he isn't a resident here. There must be somebody else in charge. Is that fellow fat?"

"Dr. Haas?" Sudema thought. "He's sort of regular:'
"Tall?"

"Regular," the lieutenant said again. "Ordinary looking, even though he's got all these PhDs in science and all, but likable nevertheless, I thought. The State Security fellows had a long talk with him, they were rather impressed."

"Why?" De Gier asked. "You just described him as regular. Regularity is hardly impressive."

"Looks don't always matter, Sergeant."

Grijpstra patted Sudema's shoulder. "I'm glad you say that. That's the sergeant's trouble, he doesn't penetrate beyond the outside layer. Like with that lady just now. Did you see him gape? Biased De Gier could never consider her as a suspect. She immediately, because she happens to look fertile and warm, changes into some sort of goddess in his immature mind. When there are beautiful people around, I may as well forget about De Gier. He becomes a dead weight that I have to drag around. Disgusting. Quite."

"That lady is no suspect," the lieutenant said sternly.

"Why are we standing here?" De Gier asked. "That's the greenhouse over there. This is some garden by the way." He looked around.

"Just look at the placement of these rocks. Makes you think you're surrounded by mountains. Very foreign."

"Exactly," the lieutenant said. "The ninja feller was hiding here, behind this little artificial hill. He crouched down, waiting for Dzung to move about in the greenhouse over there. Because of the warm weather, the windows were open, but as you can see the view is somewhat obstructed by all those flowering plants in there. The killer waited patiently, right here."

"Orchids," De Gier said, "Lee Dzung was growing beautiful orchids. This is an elegant place. Maybe Chinese heaven looks like this. Wasn't he smart, this Mr. Dzung?"

"Okay," Sudema said. "Dzung was moving about inside the greenhouse. The killer is waiting for his chance. He throws the. . .hmmm. . .well, he threw it, jumped over that outside wall and was gone. Nobody saw him. The gardener was on the other side of the greenhouse. He heard Dzung fall."

"Yeh," Grijpstra said. "Smart is the word. But Dzung got killed. He got outsmarted. Pity, really. I like a man to get away with the whole thing. Just think: No taxes. Immense profits. Flies in and out in first class airplanes. Has this wonderful woman in what he considers an exotic foreign country. Plays about in surroundings that must be ideal to Chinese taste."

"As you say," Sudema said. "Dzung flew in and out. There's a Lear Jet in Amsterdam Airport, now, registered in Fiji."

"I wonder if Dzung made a will," Grijpstra said. "Who cares?" De Gier asked. "He's subject to Dutch law. Minny is legally married to the deceased so she inherits the house and whatever else he owns in Holland."

"Dzung would have known that wouldn't he?" Grijpstra asked. "He probably has other wives."

"Mistresses more likely," De Gier said. "He had to marry here so that he could have this heaven in Minny's name. If he was smart he wouldn't marry unless he had to." De Gier turned around. "What's the place worth? Just check that palace. Terraces, spires, three stories. Well-furnished I'm sure."

"Nothing but the best," the lieutenant said. "There's a Chinese, wing toward the other side, stocked with treasures. Screens and paintings and sculptures and what not. Most outlandish. Minny took me on a tour."

"A tour. . ." De Gier said, "maybe I could ask her. . ."

"None of that." Grijpstra's heavy finger poked at the sergeant's stomach. "There will be no flirtation with a suspect."

"Ah." Sudema smiled benignly. "No interference, of course. I'm taking you around, showing you this and that, discussing theories, analyzing suspicions, but this case is closed to you and to me, too. State Security took over."

Minny called from the terrace. "Tea is ready."

De Gier noticed that his hostess had changed into a modest dress and that her long hair was done up in a simple bun. There was faint make-up accentuating her large eyes, that threw him a penetrating glance from behind darkened lashes. "Poor Lee," Minny said. "He always adored himself so much wandering about in his gown, fussing with the plants, creating the illusion of a river by spreading all those pebbles. Do you know that he brought a truckload of oval pebbles in and then put them down parallel, one by one? See it there? It's coming out between those two little hills like a stream rushing out of mountains? He explained it to me; he was such an artist."

"In Chinese?" Grijpstra asked.

"In English," Minny said.

"You speak good English?"

"Some." Minny said. "I was learning."

"Did your husband often go to his factory in Dingjum?" Gijpstra asked.

Minny arranged her long slender legs, pulling up her skirt a little, then dropping it again. De Gier shivered.

"Are you cold?" Minny asked, her soft eyes expressing concern about the sergeant's involuntary shudder.

"Just impressed by your beauty," De Gier said kindly. "Did your husband take an interest in his product? Computer chips was it? Some advanced line of specialized mint goods?"

"You should see that factory," Minny said. "Everything is automated. The chips manufacture chips. The machines hum day and night and Dr. Haas watches them from a glass cage stuck to the ceiling. Dr.

Haas used to visit here from time to time and they'd work with a computer that he rigged up on the third floor. It was linked to the factory. Lee hardly ever went out."

"You know Dr. Haas well?"

"He'd come over for dinner."

"Often?"

"Yes," Minny said. "Too often, and always so late. I like to have dinner early but Haas worked until eight o'clock at night. I got bored. Chips and computers, that's what my husband and Haas always talked about. It's another language. Other languages bore me, too."

"Would you show me that stone river?" De Gier asked. "I'm fascinated. So Mr. Dzung personally arranged a million pebbles so they would look like wavelets; how poetic."

"There's a real stream on the other side of the house," Minny said, "and quite a large pond. Lee was breeding goldfish. Some are so beautiful, with all sorts of blended colors and many-finned tails."

De Gier saw the stone river first, and picked up some pebbles. He followed his hostess down a path around the main budding of the estate and squatted at the side of a pond. Minny sat next to him on an ornamental rock. "Can you make pebbles bounce off water?" De Gier asked. "I used to be good at that when I was a kid. Maybe I can still do it" He threw a pebble with a clumsy twist of his wrist. It ricocheted once and sank.

"That wasn't so good," Minny said. "Let me try, too."

All Minny's pebbles splashed and disappeared. "Maybe they aren't the right pebbles," De Gier said, staring discreetly at Minny's slim ankles. "Were you really happy with Lee?"

He thought she moved closer, for her hand almost touched his. "Yes," Minny said. "I like older men. My father left my mother when I was small so I'm probably frustrated. Lee was over forty."

"I'm thirty-nine," De Gier said.

She straightened her dress down her legs. "You look younger."

"I'll be forty next month." The sergeant got up and extended a hand. She held on to him and allowed herself to be lifted. They walked along and reached a lawn that stretched to the far fence. A tennis ball had been left on the path. "That's Poopy's ball," Minny said. "Poopy is my terrier. Lee didn't like the dog; it would dig holes in all his funny gardens. Poopy is staying with my sister now."

De Gier picked up the ball and ran out to the lawn. "Catch." She jumped but the ball whizzed by her and hit the house. It came bouncing back. De Gier put up a slow hand and missed it, too.

Grijpstra and Sudema appeared. "Come and see me sometime," Minny said into the sergeant's ear. "It gets lonely here. But please, phone me first."

"Sure," De Gier smiled. 'Thank you for the tea," he said loudly. "And for letting us see the gardens. I envy you."

A maid came out of the mansion to tell Minny that the laundry machinery in the cellar wasn't working properly again. Minny said goodbye and disappeared into the house.

"Let's go, Sergeant" Grijpstra ordered briskly. De Gier glanced over his shoulder. "Just a minute." He ran back to the side-garden and picked up Poopy's ball. Released from a swing of De Gier's long arm, it hit a wall and came shooting back. He caught it without effort.

"Are you coming?" Gijpstra bellowed.

De Gier dug in his pocket and produced a pebble. The pebble was flung at the pond's surface and bounced off, and again, and again, in long graceful curves.

The sergeant came running back.

Grijpstra frowned. "Childish!"

"Heh, heh," said De Gier.

"Tell me everything," Sergeant Grijpstra said, as he waved at Sudema who was saluting them from under the plane trees that guarded his station. The lieutenant had begged to be excused for a while. His tomatoes needed their daily attention. He would be available again a little later in the day. De Gier drove around the corner, parked the VW, lit a cigarette and reported on his recent adventure.

"Okay," Grijpstra said. "You've got something there but that business about phoning her first means nothing. Maybe there's no lover as yet in Minny's life. Women hate being surprised by an erotic enthusiast suddenly appearing at the door. Minny is attractive but a quarter of her beauty is clothes, make-up, perfume and what not. She wants to smack you with the full hundred percent of her oversized dazzle; and to work that up may take her an hour."

"Wow," De Glier said.

"Beg pardon, Sergeant?"

"She's beautiful," De Gier said. "A Viking Queen. You know, you meet this absolutely stunning woman and you somehow manage to wake up next to her in the morning and you kiss her awake and you wait for the heavenly wisdom flowing out of that lovely shape, and it isn't there?"

"I have no Idea what you're talking about," Grijpstra said. "I live a quiet life. I paint tasteless pictures on my days off. Now what are you saying?"

"That," De Gier said, "I don't think Minny will be disappointing."

Gijpstra withdrew into a disagreeable silence.

"I'm," De Gier said dreamily, "telling you that Minny is capable of murder. She inspires me." He grinned at the adjutant. "To do good things, of course. But then I'm a good guy. Now what if she was involved with a bad guy, a ninja? Wouldn't she inspire him to do evil?"

Grijpstra moved his back against his seat, grunting softly. "Yeh. Maybe. So she can't throw pebbles and she can't catch balls. Why? She must have tried some sports. All schools have games. She looks athletic."

"Did you notice that her left eye tends to drift somewhat?" De Gier asked. "She may have trouble focusing especially when she's tired. These last days must have been a strain."

"Let's go," Grijpstra said. "We stayed in a hotel in Dingjum once, that time we were here before. An old-fashioned inn. Think you can find it again?"

The innkeeper remembered the two Chinese visitors who came for Mr. Dzung. "Mr. Wang and Mr. Tzu. Their full names and addresses are in the register; let me look them up."

"You checked their passports?" Grijpstra asked.

The innkeeper nodded. "I always do."

De Gier noted the names and addresses on his pad. Both Chinese originated in Taipeh.

"They were older men," the innkeeper said. "Quite pleasant."

"Athletic?" De Gier asked.

The innkeeper laughed. "Not really. I have a mini golf course in the back and they puttered about; they weren't too good."

"And where did they go from here?"

"Let's see now," the innkeeper said. "Wait a minute. Maybe I do know. They phoned Philips Electronics; I remember because they couldn't find the right number and there was some trouble with the operator, it seemed. I helped them out. They were supposed to meet someone there and we couldn't locate the fellow, but they did talk to him in the end."

"So you think they left for Philips Headquarters from here?"

"Yes," the innkeeper said. "I remember now. They had a rented car and my wife helped them to trace a route on the map."

"Can we use the phone?" De Gier asked. "It would help if you remembered the name of the man at Philips."

De Gier dialed. "Sir? A Mr. Wang and a Mr. Tzu, are they still around?"

He listened. "They're in Amsterdam now?" He thanked his informant and replaced the phone.

"Back again?" Sudema asked. "I thought I was rid of you. I beg your pardon. Always happy to entertain colleagues, of course. Especially when they don't interfere. You wouldn't be interfering, would you now?"

"You know, lieutenant," Grijpstra said, "I do admire you. You said that Minny wasn't a suspect and, by jove, she isn't."

"Not a direct murder suspect," De Gier said. "No, sir!"

"And you did express doubts about those two Chinese," Grijpstra said, "You and I both know what State Security is like. A bunch of old dodderers wandering about their Victorian offices looking for a lost slipper. They actually managed to come out here?"

"Briefly," Sudema said. "They talked to Dr. Haas and wrote their report. They also checked out some shipments of chips that were sent to Germany and probably reached Moscow."

"And what is Dr. Haas going to do, now that his boss is dead?"

Sudema rolled a cigarette and studied its ends. He tapped the cigarette on his desk. "Yes, Adjutant, I know. I'm perhaps not quite as foolish as you city slicker chaps may be thinking. There could be a possible connection there. Minny has talked to her lawyer and it seems pretty clear that the factory is now hers. It may be an affiliated company to the Fiji tax-free head office, and linked to Taipeh, but according to Dr. Haas, all the patents are in Lee Dzung's name and Minny will probably inherit them outright, too."

De Gier rolled a cigarette, too, and imitated Sudema's careful treatment of the ends, "If that lawyer knows his job, Minny stands a chance of getting hold of all Dzung's assets."

Sudema blew a little smoke to the station's rustic ceiling and admired its age-old beams. "Minny didn't kill Dzung."

Grijpstra peeled a cigar out of plastic. "You know, Lieutenant, I would just love to watch you while you make monkeys out of State Security. I could never stand seeing those nincompoops waste the taxpayers' money. Do you have any idea about the size of their budget?"

"I saw the Mercedes limousine they parked in front of this station," Sudema said. He hit the desk. "Do you know that they wouldn't eat at our restaurant here? They said they didn't care for tomato salad. They actually preferred to go back to Amsterdam and some fancy bodega. It took them three and a half hours to get back here again."

"I think we should go and see Dr. Haas sometime," De Gier said, "and perhaps you can come along, Lieutenant, I know how busy you are but this might be worth it. As an officer you don't need us to sign the final report with you. We weren't really here, anyway; we were just passing through as we happened to be in the neighborhood."

"I do," Sudema said, "sometimes read the weekly magazines. We're dealing with Taiwan Chinese. You mentioned that Dzung was a smart guy. I agree. The Taiwan authorities probably squeezed Dzung in Taipeh. Imagine—here is a genius who comes up with a superb product and he makes an immense profit. Who runs Taiwan? Generals and so forth, corrupt warlords who escaped from the communist mainland. So Dzung thinks of a way in which he can have his noodles with sauce and eat them, too. Maybe he sold his stuff from here to Russia out of spite."

"How did he get Minny? Grijpstra asked.

"My guess is as good as yours, Adjutant."

"Let the sergeant guess." Grijpstra pushed De Gier's shoulder.

"Share your knowledge of the world, De Gier."

"Me?" De Gier looked up. "Escort service, I would imagine. Dzung came here, he set up his operation with Dr. Haas. He probably found Haas through some technical paper. All these top-notch scientists correspond, meet at congresses, get together on schemes. Haas Introduced Dzung to an organization that rents out attractive females. Dzung selected the very best. Haas suggested marriage and Minny was willing. She preferred to be legal."

Sudema rolled another perfect cigarette. "Yes, I think so, too, and there may be some risk there: Minny obviously benefits by her husband's death. Dr. Haas does not. For one thing, he's married and has some kids. He strikes me as a scientist, not as a businessman. Dzung is the genius, not Haas. And. . ." Sudema was admiring the beams of his ceiling again, "lets face it, Dutchmen aren't killers. The Taiwanese are. If Dzung was selling superchips to the Russians, the Americans would lean on the generals of Taipeh. . ."

"Who would send thugs, ninjas, lithe louts trained in bizarre murderous methods," Grijpstra said, sucking his cigar contentedly. The CIA must be pleased that Dzung caught that steel star in his neck. But I still think all this is very far fetched. Now what if there were no assassins? Not from Taipeh anyway? Now suppose you could prove that? Wouldn't that be great? A feather in your hat?"

"I think I could help," De Gier said.

"Please do," the lieutenant said, "I'm very fond of feathers."

Grijpstra got up. "I could save you some time. You drive to Amsterdam with my sergeant and I'll visit this Dr. Haas. When you come back you can tie things up."

"You wouldn't interfere now?" Sudema asked. "Right, Adjutant?"

"Never," Grijpstra said. "Just tell me where I can find the good doctor."

"You're not coming through very clearly," the operator at the radio room of Amsterdam Municipal Headquarters said.

De Gier frowned at the small microphone in his hand. "As long as you can hear me. I'm looking for a Mr. Tzu and a Mr. Wang, staying in a hotel in Amsterdam; could you check which hotel I should go to and let me know within the next half hour?"

"Will try. Over and out."

The VW was speeding along the Great Dike and approaching the capital. Sudema had been watching swans on the lake. He glanced at De Gier's handsome profile. "Shouldn't we call for an arrest team? I'm a fairly good shot but my book on martial arts says that a good thrower of. . .what the hell, what do you call those things again?"

"*Shuriken*, Lieutenant?"

"Right. That a good thrower of those damned things can fling a dozen in no time at all. It'll be like a barrage from an automatic rifle."

"Nah," De Gier said.

"Suit yourself," Sudema said. "I hear you won the prizes at the national police unarmed combat contest this year. Can you catch those whatdoyoucallums?"

"Forget unarmed combat," De Gier said. "Nothing beats a gun. Make sure that they can't reach you with any part of their bodies and shoot to kill in case of doubt. Don't complain and explain later. Self-defense is still a good excuse." He grinned at the lieutenant. "Don't worry about the present situation though."

"You're pretty sure, eh, Sergeant?"

"I don't think Wang and Tzu are assassins," De Gier said. "If I did, I would probably ask for assistance. I'm not really a hero, you know. I have to go home and feed my cat. There're some books I'd still like to read, and perhaps I'll meet a lady sometime who'll look like Minny."

"Not Minny herself? I think you'd be welcome."

"Wouldn't that be nice?" De Gier asked. "And wander about in that exotic abode the morning after? Breakfast on the terrace? If she really baked those cookies that came with the tea, herself, she'll be a good cook, too."

The lieutenant smiled happily. "And she isn't a dumb blonde either."

"Intelligence goes both ways," De Gier said. The radio crackled.

"Sergeant de Gier?"

"Right here."

"Your parties are staying at the Victoria Hotel. We checked with the desk and they are in their room. Should I tell them to expect you?"

"Please," De Gier said. He pushed the microphone back under the dashboard.

"We aren't being silly, now?" Sudema asked. "If we are, I might want to phone my wife."

De Gier unhooked the microphone. "Headquarters? De Gier again. Please phone the State Police station at Dingjum, Friesland, and tell the constable to phone Lieutenant Sudema's wife to tell her that her husband may be late for dinner."

"Thanks," Sudema said.

De Gier shook hands, Lieutenant Sudema saluted.

"Please sit down," Mr. Wang said.

"Cup of tea?" Mr. Tzu asked. He poured. The four men raised their cups and smiled politely at each other.

"We're sorry to hear about Mr. Dzung's death," Wang said.

"Very sorry. To die in a foreign country is unpleasant experience. Perhaps his body can go home, yes?"

"If a request is made," Sudema said, "I'm sure we would be happy to oblige. To be murdered is also an unpleasant experience."

"Very sad," Tzu said. Tzu stooped and a hearing aid hid in the tufted white hairs sprouting from his ear. He also wore thick glasses. Wang's belly rested comfortably on his thighs. Wang would be a little younger than Tzu.

"We represent Mustang Electrics," Wang said. "We deal in advanced computer technology. Mr. Dzung and Dr. Haas are known to us and we thought that Dzung might help us to do business with Phllips, on commission, of course."

"Or take over our idea," Tzu said, "for money, but he wasn't interested. So, instead, we made contact with Philips directly."

"Successfully?" De Gier asked.

"Hopefully," Wang said. "Likely," Tzu said. "Very likely, yes; our suggestions were well received."

"We hear," De Gier said, smiling apologetically, "that you and Mr. Tzu did, eh, disagree with Mr. Dzung while visiting him in Dinjum? There was, perhaps, some expression of anger during your brief get-together?"

"Hmm?" Wang asked. He spoke in Chinese to Tzu. Tzu shook his head.

"No," Wang said. "Not at all. It's very rude to be angry with a business relation. Besides, it doesn't pay."

Tzu polished his glasses with the tip of his tie. "Now, who would have told you that Dzung and us had disagreement?"

De Gier reached absentmindedly for his teaspoon but his movement was awkward and the spoon slithered across the table into Wang's lap. The sergeant apologized. "Hmm?" Wang asked.

"Sorry, sir, I dropped my spoon on your side."

Wang picked up the spoon with some effort as he had to bend down. He gave it back.

"Talking about Dr. Haas," De Gier said, "you say you knew him. Dr. Haas was in Taiwan, perhaps?"

Tzu nodded. "Oh yes, for many years. Quite an expert on things Chinese. Very bright, this Dr. Haas."

"Like what things Chinese?" Lieutenant Sudema asked.

Tzu replaced his glasses. "Chinese table tennis. He was very good. He beat my twice-removed nephew, an expert in Kong Fu."

"Kong Fu equates with table-tennis?" De Gier asked.

Wang smiled. "No."

"Many-sided man this Dr. Haas," Tzu whispered.

De Gier smiled over the rim of his cup. "And what are you doing in Amsterdam now?"

Wang smiled broadly. "Very little, Sergeant. Bit of a holiday. The negotiations with Philips were straightforward, no time was wasted so now we waste it here a few days of..."

"Museums," Mr. Tzu said.

"Museums, Sergeant," Wang nodded enthusiastically.

De Gier got up. "I hope you're enjoying your stay in the city." He stumbled as he went to shake Mr. Tzu's hand. Mr. Tzu tried to move away but bumped heavily against a chair. Sudema steadied De Gier's sliding body.

"I'm sorry," De Gier said.

"My fault entirely," Tzu said smiling.

Grijpstra was waiting at the State Police station. De Gier bounded through the door. "That didn't take long did it? Did you see Dr. Haas?"

"I did," Grijpstra said. "Lieutenant Sudema? Sir?"

Sudema snapped to attention. "Yes. Adjutant at your orders. I hope we didn't hold you up."

"Lieutenant," Grijpstra said heavily, "why didn't you tell me that Dr. Haas has an alibi."

Sudema slid behind his desk and threw his cap at a hook attached to the wall. The cap missed the hook. "I didn't? I thought I had."

De Gier sat down "A good alibi?"

"Pretty good, Sergeant." Grijpstra smiled sadly. "We may have wasted time and effort. What were your Chinese ninjas like?"

"They never threw any steel stars, I would think." De Gier stretched. "Boy I'm surprised we weren't caught for speeding. A hundred miles an hour all the way up that wonderful straight dike. Wasn't that fun, Lieutenant?"

"Yes," Sudema said. "I rather agree with your sergeant, Grijpstra. Maybe Wang and Tzu are excellent actors but I would think they're what they say they are, businessmen trying to make a profit and at present, have a little holiday in sexy Amsterdam."

"They're clumsy," De Gier said. "Definitely no sportsmen. Uncoordinated movements and entirely unaware of their physical positions. They couldn't drop a brick on a rabbit in a trap."

"Could Dr. Haas do better?" Sudema asked.

Grijpstra arranged his hands on his stomach and slid a little further down into his chair. "Yes:'

"You tested him?" De Gier asked.

"Dr. Haas," Grijpstra said ponderously, "is an agile athlete. A fly buzzed by him and he caught it with two fingers without paying much attention. I threw him my lighter and he plucked it from the air. I bumped him on the staircase and I swear he was ready to do a somersault and drop to the landing below on his feet."

"But he didn't throw a *shuriken* at Mr. Dzung?" De Gier asked. "Isn't that hard to believe?"

"Wasn't Dzung killed at eleven-o-five AM, last Friday morning?" Grijpstra asked.

"Yes," Sudema said brightly.

"At that time, Dr. Haas claims he was in his office and," Grijpstra said as he raised a menacing finger, "he produced two witnesses to prove that fact." His finger dropped to accuse Sudema. "You never told me that."

"The beeper stuff?" Sudema asked. "State Security believed it. Why shouldn't I?"

"So why didn't you tell me?"

"I forgot," Sudema said. "Adjutant, you're in the country now. We're all bumpkins here, vegetating in rustic retardation."

Grijpstra's hand became a fist that shook and trembled. "No sir. You didn't believe that beeper stuff yourself and you're testing me now. Am I right? Confess."

Sudema bowed his head. "I believed the alibi at the time, but later I wondered, and when you came here to shine your dazzling light, I thought I might not mention the detail to see what you might make of it."

"What beeper stuff?" De filer asked.

"Bah," Grijstra said. "You know about beepers, Sergeant. A gadget you keep in your pocket and it beeps when you're wanted. So you run along and find out what you're wanted for. They use beepers at Dzung's computer factory. Some of the employees wander about and may be out of reach of a phone so they get beeped and respond."

"At eleven AM last Friday, Dr. Haas beeped two of his wandering employees?" De Gier asked.

"And they both answered by phone," Grijspstra said. "They made use of inside phones connected to Dr. Haas' center of command. He spoke to them, gave them instructions, listened to their comments, commented on their comments—there were conversations. Both employees confirm that fact. Dr. Haas provided himself with a very nice alibi, all right."

"Can you crack it?" Sudema asked, "Dr. Haas was very confident when State Security questioned him as to his whereabouts at the time of Dzung's death. Too confident, maybe?"

"Now the lieutenant tells us," Grijpstra complained.

"You weren't here at the time," Sudema said.

"Grijpstra?" De Gier asked. "Can you crack that alibi or not? If you can't, we're going home. I've got to feed my cat sometime. She's waiting for me at my apartment right now."

Grijpstra took off his coat and waistcoat. He linked his fingers behind striped suspenders and began to pace the floor, Sudema stared.

"He's thinking," De Gier said. "Would you like to help? Are you wearing suspenders?"

"Are you?" Sudema asked.

"I'm not," De Gier said, "but maybe you can lend me a pair."

Sudema opened a wardrobe, took a pair of suspenders from his spare uniform, and passed it to De Gier. De Gier snapped them to his trousers. He nodded to the lieutenant. Lieutenant Sudema took off his uniform jacket and slid his hands behind the narrow strips that kept up his pants. "Like this? You are both crazy! Am I humoring you properly?"

"When conventional methods fail," De Gier said, "and time presses, we explore the beyond. You don't mind dancing a little now, do you?"

"Oh shit," Sudema said, "Do I have to?"

"THINK," Grijpstra roared, interrupting his self-induced trance. "THINK, IF YOU PLEASE."

"THINK," shouted De Gier.

"Think," squeaked the lieutenant.

They walked in a circle, chanting "Think," Grijpstra sonorously, De Gier in a normal voice, and the lieutenant in a falsetto. The constable from the office next door came in to see if everything was all right. The contemplators ignored him. The constable withdrew, whistling his disbelief. He whistled rhythmically, in time with the chant.

Grijpstra skipped his feet at every fourth measure. De Gier did likewise. The lieutenant imitated his examples. The dance didn't take long. Grijpstra stopped at his chair and sat down. De Gier dropped down on the next chair. Sudema hopped behind his desk.

"That must have done it." Grijpstra said. "You first, Sergeant. Did anything occur"

"Let's hear the lieutenant," De Gier said, "Our method is new to him and may have worked spectacularly on his unsuspecting brain. What thoughts popped up, sir?"

"I thought," Sudema said dreamily, "that Dr. Haas is a computer expert. He analyzes what goes on in normal communication, then apes it with his machines. All communication can be analyzed and classsified."

"Foreseen?" Grijpstra asked. "Programmed into a phone at proper intervals?"

"But," De Gier said, "not when the communication is too complicated. The number of possible responses to a given question is fairly large, and one response to one question wouldn't even satisfy a numbskull of State Security. There would have to be several responses, and responses to the responses, and proper timing of them all."

"Ah," Sudema said. He patted the top of his desk. "Ah. Now I know what bothered me when Dr. Haas presented his alibi. Both workers who were willing to swear that they responded to his beeping, and subsequently communicated with him, proving thereby that Haas was in his office, were numbskulls."

"Are numbskulls employed by a factory turning out superchips for advanced computers?" De Gier asked.

Sudema waved a hand. "The two witnesses were of the fetch-and-carry variety. They open and close heavy boxes, put them on trucks, or take them off trucks as the case may be; that sort of thing. They were usually busy outside the main building, running about between storage sheds; thats why they carried beepers."

"So," Grijpstra said, "Dr. Haas would give them simple commands. First he beeps them. They run to the nearest phone and dial the chief's number. He answers. 'Hello.'"

"Yes," De Gier said, "and the man says, 'Hi boss, it's me, Frank,' and Haas says, 'Hi, Frank, would you carry box X from storage station Z,' and Frank says, 'There are no more boxes X, boss.'"

"Right," Sudema said, "and Haas says, 'Sure, Frank, there's still a box X in shed A, in the rear.'"

Grijpstra rubbed his hands. "Yes. But Frank might be saying more than he is expected to say; the message becomes longer, and if Haas gives his pre-recorded answer, it cuts into what Frank has to say and Frank becomes bewildered."

Sudema rubbed his hands, too. "And Frank wasn't, right? Frank testified to me and the State Security yoyos that he was conducting a normal conversation with Dr. Haas while the very same Dr. Haas, our athletic friend who kills flies on the wing between thumb and finger, was throwing a, what do you call it again?"

"*Shuriken?*" De Gier asked.

"Yep," Sudema nodded vigorously. "No matter, however. Dr. Haas holds PhDs in science. He must have used a device that wouldn't permit his pre-recorded messages, commands, orders, to get into the phone before the line was void of Franks response."

Lieutenant Sudema sighed. "Pretty tricky."

De Gier shrugged. "Isn't Dr. Haas supposed to be a wizard? He's got a factory filled with tricky equipment. Surely it won't be too difficult for him to devise a gadget that wouldn't let the recorded messages out before Frank could finish phrasing his simple comments?"

Grijpstra rubbed out his soggy cigar butt. "Listen, Lieutenant, Frank and the other witness who holds up Dr. Haas' alibi, are predictable men. Dr. Haas was their boss so they wouldn t gab too much at him. First he gives them an order, then they say that it can't be done. Haas knows that, beforehand. He has manipulated the situation. His device waited for Frank, or the other feller, to stop talking, and then released another pre-recorded message in Dr. Haas' voice. He tells them that they are mistaken and that they can obey his order if they do this or that. They say, 'Yes, sir,' and hang up. Thinking back, it may seem to them that they had quite a conversation."

De Gier checked his watch. "It's getting late. Minny says that Dr. Haas likes to work late, but he may, by now, be ready to leave his office. Are we doing something? If not, I'd rather go back. I ve got to feed my cat."

"Would you," Grijpstra asked Sudema, "own one of those mini-cassette players that also records?"

Sudema jumped up, rushed across his office, yanked the door open and pointed accusingly at the constable reclining behind his desk. "Ha!"

The constable was listening to his cassette player, connected to his ears by tiny phones. "Give," Sudema barked, holding out his hand. "And find me a spare tape."

He ran back. "Here you are, Adjutant."

Grijpstra explained. Sudema applauded. "Clever," De Gier said, raising his eyebrows. "Amazing. You thought of that yourself?"

"Sit in the corner there," Grijpstra said, "and fill up that tape. You may not be equipped with a lot of furniture upstairs but you are a good actor."

De Gier spoke into the cassette recorder. Grijpstra put on his waistcoat and jacket. Sudema practiced fast draws with his pistol.

"Now," Grijpstra said. "That sounds fine. Return the lieutenant's suspenders and go talk to the constable. Make sure that he knows what to do."

Sudema's gun was stuck again in its holster. He yanked it free. "Pow!" He pointed it at a cupboard. He shook his head. "Can't we give this thing a little time? I could call in an arrest team."

"Nah," Grijpstra said.

"Gentlemen," Dr. Haas said. "I was just on my way out. You might not have caught me."

"You're using the right verb." Grijpstra said in a cold menacing voice. "You're under arrest, sir. Anything you say from now on, we'll most definitely use against you. Isn't that right Lieutenant?"

"Absolutely," Sudema said. "You're ordered, Dr. Haas, to return to your office forthwith. I, a ranking officer of the State Police, accuse you of foully murdering your employer, Lee Dzung. A despicable deed for which you will be tried in due course."

"You're joking," Dr. Haas said bravely. He looked at De Gier.

De Gier arranged his face into an expression of stern contempt.

"Sergeant," Grijpstra said, "you can go outside and guard the building."

De Gier turned and left.

"Now," Sudema said, "let's not waste time. Back to your office, sir, where you can confess to your heinous crime."

Dr. Haas sat down in his office. The lieutenant and Grijpstra looked at him expectantly. "Are you crazy?" Dr. Haas said. "What are you trying to do? What *is* this charade? *Me* kill my good friend, Lee? My beneficent employer?"

"Your alibi is not good," Sudema barked. "You never fooled *us*,

I'll have you know. Anyone can turn rings around State Security, dear sir. Espionage? Foreign killers? Selling of contraband killing machines to the red devils lurking nearby? Ha!" Sudema laughed harshly for a while.

"You're dealing with the Police now," Grijpstra said. "The State Police. The lieutenant saw through your ruse from the start."

Dr. Haas smiled. "Really, Adjutant. I can prove to you that quite a lot of equipment left this factory with a dubious destination. I warned Lee many a time. I'm sorry he died, of course, but he had it coming. Believe me, the Taiwanese Secret Service doesn't play around. You underestimate our State Security, too. Once they knew what was on, they wisely decided not to pursue the matter."

Grijpstra peeled a cigar. He looked up. "Bah. Really, Dr. Haas. I'm a police officer, too. Your true motivations can be spelled out easily enough. What were you after? Money? How to get it? Well now. . .?" Grijpstra sucked smoke. "Well now, my crafty doctor, you seduced poor Minny, arranged to divorce your wife, promised Minny you would marry her, planned to procure Mr. Dzung's millions that way."

"What would I want with Minny?" Dr. Haas shouted.

"Leaving out the pornography," Sudema said quietly, "we know exactly what you'd like to do to the hapless girl. A sex object framed in pure gold?"

Dr. Haas folded his arms. "I do have an alibi, Lieutenant. You've heard it before and the judge will hear it, too. I beg you, for your own sake, not to make an idiot out of yourself."

The phone rang. Dr. Haas picked it up. "Who? Sergeant de Gier? Who's Sergeant de Gier?"

The voice on the phone said he was the tall man with the magnificent mustache whom Dr. Haas had just met. "I see," Dr. Haas said. "What do you want? I'm busy."

The voice said that he wanted Dr. Hass to confess to killing Lee Dzung, a multimillionaire, so that he could marry Mrs. Dzung and collect the multimillions."

"You're out of your poor mind." snarled Dr. Haas.

The voice on the phone said that he was out of the phone and that, in fact, he was coming into Dr. Haas' office.

De Gier walked into the room. "See?"

Dr. Haas looked at De Gier.

The voice on the phone said that it was surprising, was it not? How could Dr. Haas be speaking to Sergeant de Gier on the phone while Sergeant de Gier was standing right before him? Now wasn't that weird?

Dr. Haas slammed down the phone.

Silence filled the office.

"How did you do that?" Dr. Haas finally asked.

"You know how," Lieutenant Sudema said darkly. "Same way you fabricated your alibi. We don't have your advanced equipment so we used my constable to make the call and to activate the recorder at the appropriate moments. The device you have around will be tracked down by experts. Should be easy enough. Your proof will be destroyed."

Dr. Haas hid his face in his hands.

"Or you can show it to us now," Grijpstra said kindly. "It'll shorten your agony, poor man."

"You pathetic asshole," De Gier said kindly. "Minny doesn't love you anyway. You would have lost without our non-interference. What a risk to take." The sergeant spread his hands. "You really think she would go for you. She thinks you're boring. What a senseless rigmarole you set up. You merely did her a service that she planned you to perform. You really think Minny would hand you the loot?"

"Poor sucker," Sudema whispered.

"She abused you," Grijpstra said, nodding sadly.

Dr. Haas dropped his hands. "Minny loves me as much as I love her. I liberated that poor innocent girl. We'll be happy together for ever after."

"Yes?" De Gier asked. "You were planning to see her tonight?"

Dr. Haas glared at the sergeant.

Grijpstra jumped up. "At what time?" Grijpstra roared. He sat down heavily again. "Not that it matters, as she won't be seeing you. Even at such short notice, with Mr. Dzung turning in his recently dug grave, she's soliciting another lover."

"Not you," Sudema said helpfully. "Oh, no?"

"Impossible!" Dr. Haas grabbed the phone. De Gier's hand grabbed the doctor's wrist. "Allow me, sir," De Gier said. "I'll make that call. What's her number?"

Dr. Haas mumbled the number. De Gier dialed, "Minny?" De Gier asked shyly. "It's me, Rinus de Gier. The sergeant you played ball with this afternoon. Remember?"

"Oh, Rinus," Minny moaned.

Grijpstra sneaked up to the phone. He pressed a button on its side. Minny's voice became audible to all parties concerned.

"Of course I remember," Minny said weakly.

"I was wondering," De Gier said. "I'm supposed to stay in Dingjum tonight. Not on what I came to see you about this afternoon, that's all over now. I was just wondering. . ."

"Oh, do come," Minny said. "That would be nice. I'm so lonely in this big house. Could you see me in an hour or so? I do want to receive you in style."

Grijpstra smiled gleefully at Sudema. Sudema winked back. Dr. Haas listened with round eyes.

"I'll be there," De Gier said. "Goodbye, dear Minny."

"Goodbye Rinus," Minny said softly. "Thanks for calling."

De Gier replaced the phone.

Grijpstra rubbed his hands while looking at the doctor.

"See? You got trapped in your own greed. She has no use for you now that Mr. Dzung's vast wealth is available to her. She'll have the time of her life with more attractive men."

"You may be smart, Doctor," Lieutenant Sudema said, "but your looks are regular, to say the least. You really thought that a beauty queen would fall for you?" Sudema laughed harshly.

The phone rang. Dr. Haas picked it up. Minny's voice once again penetrated to the far corners of the office. "Haas? Listen, Haas, something came up. I don't want to see you tonight. Okay?"

"But Minny," Haas said. "Please, we have an appointment; there's so much to discuss; our future. . ."

"What future?" Minny asked shrilly. "Perhaps you should never come to see me again. If you do, you might be in trouble."

"Minny?" Dr. Baas shrieked. The phone clicked dryly.

"Now, make your confession," Sudema said briskly. "Let's get this over with."

Dr. Haas looked at the blotter on his desk. His face became calm.

His deeply recessed eyes behind the gold-rimmed spectacles began to sparkle. A smile pushed up the corners of his thin lips.

"What's up?" Grijpstra asked.

"If you won't talk," Sudema said, "I have to remind you that you are under arrest. Please stand up, turn and face the wall with your hands above your head. Spread your legs, Dr. Haas. I have to frisk you now."

Dr. Haas smiled. "Just a minute, Lieutenant. Let's go through this again. What did I do?"

"You killed a man, Doctor," Sudema said.

"I exterminated a dangerous criminal," Dr. Haas corrected. "A flaw in our society who suppiled the enemy with lethal machinery that will be used to do away with the free world. I also removed an alien sadist who beat up one of the most beautiful women with a whip spilt in seven thongs. I saved both democracy and a rare specimen of local female beauty. Is that a crime?"

"Sure," De Gler said. "Undemocratic, too. Did you ask for a vote?"

Dr. Haas kept smiling. "You're such joker, Sergeant. Allow me to finish my plea. If you arrest me, nothing is gained and much will be lost. Maybe Minny will get the present available loot, and good luck to her, I say. Dzung's wealth will soon be replaced. I have, together with the wicked alien, developed an almost unimaginable improvement that will make intercontinental missiles all-seeing. Only I know how these inventions work. Let me go free and I will set up a fresh company that will control patents I can apply for alone. All three of you will be my partners. Your Investment only involves your friendship and, in return, I'll hand over ten percent of the shares. My millions will soon be made. I assure you, the profits of our new venture will be immense."

"And Minny?" Sudema asked.

"Who cares about Minny?" Dr. Haas asked.

"Have her," Dr. Haas presented Minny to De Gier on the palm of his hand. "You're so clever, Sergeant, maybe you can marry her, too. It would be nice if you can bring in some of our present equipment. It will save me some time."

"Won't Minny be a problem?" De Gier asked.

"How could she be, Sergeant? It was she who suggested I do

away with Lee. As an accomplice she'll have to stay mum."

"A bribe?" Sudema asked. Grijpstra kicked him gently. "Ah," Sudema said. "Well maybe not."

"You wouldn't want to see Minny waste away in jail" De Gier said, "would you Lieutenant?"

Sudema grinned helpfully. "Absolutely not. But only ten percent for me and you get Minny too. . ."

"Weren't you married?" De Gier asked. "Of course, you could ignore that illusionary bond—not too often, of course—and if you happened to share a growing experience with my wife and if I was away that evening spending a million here or there. . ."

The lieutenants left eyelid trembled nervously. "You mean you wouldn't mind?"

"I spent my formative years in Amsterdam," De Gier said.

Dr. Haas looked up. "Let's be serious, gentlemen." He turned to De Gier. "And would you mind sitting down, Sergeant? You make me nervous. When I was in the Far East I practiced some of the martial arts and if there's one thing I learned it was the art of always being aware. Now let's go through this again. I'm a scientist, too, and my mind is trained to make optimal use of any available situation." He smiled at his audience. "For mutual benefit of course; it's the object of science to make this a better world. I could raise my offer to fifteen percent to the lieutenant and adjutant and nothing extra for the sergeant provided he marries Minny. If not. . ." The doctor made an appeasing gesture. ". . .well that's fine too. The sergeant gets fifteen percent, too. Money, and a lot of it, will flow in either case."

"You *are* a businessman," Grijpstra said. "We were misinformed."

"Interesting," Sudema said.

De Gier moved toward a chair. "I agree. Shall we call it a deal? The sooner I can free myself from my tedious present routine. . ." He looked at Dr. Haas. The doctor wasn't paying attention. De Gier turned and leaped. Grijpstra's gun pointed at Dr. Haas. Sudema was still trying to yank his pistol free.

Both Dr. Haas' hands fled under his jacket. "HEY!" shouted De Gier. His flat hands hit the doctor's wrists. One came back and flew out again, this time against the doctor's chin. The doctor tumbled out of his chair and De Gier fell on top of him. The sergeants nimble hands quickly frisked the doctor's body. De Gier got up holding several metal stars in each hand.

Dr. Haas was coming to. Sudema gave up trying to get to his pistol, rolled the suspect over, yanked his arms to the rear and connected them with handcuffs.

The constable was waiting at the State Police station. He waved his cassette recorder. "Did I do all right?" "Splendid Job," Sudema said. "Now you know why I allowed you to listen to Beethoven during office hours. I knew your gadget would come in handy one day. Lock up this suspect, Constable. Be careful, he's a dangerous gent."

"Well," De Gier said, "we'd better drive back while there's still light. We can watch cormorants land on the lake at sunset. Didn't we have an instructive day? I thank you, Lieutenant, for showing us the way you work."

"What about my report?" Sudema asked.

"You don't need us for mere paperwork," Grijpstra said. "Suspect will provide you with a detailed confession. You made the arrest. There's circumstantial evidence; those star shaped discs, for instance."

"We don't want to interfere," De Gier said. "Are you coming, Grijpstra?"

Sudema blocked the door. "We still have to catch Minny."

"She's all yours," De Gier said. "Bring her in, confront her with Dr. Haas. They'll yell at each other. Their mutual accusations will add to evidence. That's all normal routine."

"But she's waiting for you, dolled up and all." Sudema patted the sergeants shoulder. "You bring her in, Sergeant, after you've reaped your reward. Your chief and I will be at my house having a late supper."

"I have to go," De Gier said. "I'm really not very good with women. My cat is female, too; she wipes the floor with me. I might release your suspect and interfere with your case."

"Don't want to interfere with your routine here, sir," Grijpstra said, pushing the lieutenant gently aside. "Thanks for the lunch. Your tomato salad was very tasty."

Espionage, 1989

A Law Student

Whoever dines at Amsterdam's pricey restaurant, The Plumgarden, set off by palm trees in brass buckets under a cupola ceiling wherein angels make music, whoever enjoys *nouvelle cuisine* dishes there, sprinkled with rare wines, hardly expects the gent at the next table to fall over and die.

The gent was in perfect health just a moment ago, in his tailored Homme de Ville suit. He was about to bite into caviar on fresh toast when his handsome head flopped over. Blood dribbled from his mouth and over he went, sliding slowly off his chair, then falling outright. Was he playacting? Trying to amuse his beautiful lady friend? Had he smeared tomato ketchup on his mouth? Was he about to get up again, laugh, and sip champagne? Or was this a small accident? The gent had chewed on a piece of gravel that somehow got into the caviar and broke a tooth. Being allergic to the taste of blood, he fainted. That's what it was.

Nevertheless, a calamity. The maitre de was about to appear, rightfully upset, to offer sincere apologies and tell the gent that the meal was on the house—and the dentist's bill, too. So sorry, Sir.

But why wasn't the gent getting up? Why did he insist on hugging the marble tiles of the floor?

He had been overheard to speak impeccable British just now, complete with the slight stutter that Englishmen affect before getting into a sentence and just before finishing it off. Not that he was true British—he was too dark-skinned for that. A Middle Eastern gent he would be, and very handsome for sure. As good-looking as his lady friend. The lady was most attractive indeed, in her loosely fitting jersey and tight Italian skirt. Maybe she was a model.

Well, we have to face it now—the gent is dead. The attempts of the maitre de to revive him by slapping his face gently and coaxing him back with gentle summons stopped as soon as they saw the dark stain on his satin waistcoat. What caused the dark red stain? A bullet. Had the waiter who had been serving the table, the maitre de asks, heard, perhaps, a shot?

"A what?"

The maitre stretched one finger and cocked another. "A bang?"

"No," the waiter said. "I heard a pop." He put a finger in his mouth and pulled it out.

That wasn't much help. Champagne corks have a habit of popping, and in The Plumgarden champagne corks fly about a lot.

The lady never moved. While waiters and the maitre groveled about her dainty feet she nibbled caviar, sipped some champagne. Her slender fingertips arranged her thick blonde hair.

The maitre argued with himself in French, using two voices.

"Is this a murder? *Yes*."

"Should I call in the—? *You should*."

He called the cops.

First the cops were uniformed policemen, a little later they were detectives in regular clothes: an older, fatter man with bushy grey hair and a younger, sportier type. They both had kind eyes, paleblue and darkbrown. The older man should have shaved, the younger man wore a full mustache. The older man's crumpled suit didn't fit him, the younger man's loose jacket was impeccable and his jeans cut to size.

"Who fired the shot?" Adjutant Grijpstra asked sadly, as if he knew nobody knew.

The waiter thought—he wasn't sure at all—that there had been a young, dark man around, with a shaven head. He might have been wearing light-tan trousers and a brown-leather jacket maybe. There had been considerable movement around the waiter's tables at that time. Guests were coming and going. The suspect had walked toward the table and paused. "Pop."

"Then what did he do?" the younger detective asked. He introduced himself. Rank: sergeant. Name: de Gier.

The waiter looked around. "He must have left."

The maitre felt left out. "You allowed the murderer to leave? While our guest fell into hell?"

Sergeant de Gier liked that expression. He repeated it softly. "Fell into hell." Only bad guys fall into hell. Did the maitre know the guest?

"No."

"So why 'hell'?"

"Or heaven." The maitre raised his hands to defend himself. He dropped his hands again. He himself was innocent, so did he care?

"Yes?" de Gier asked the lady.

"No," the lady whispered. Her voice vibrated—not nervously, but charmingly—while she explained that she, unfortunately, knew nothing at all. She had been looking in her bag, for she was about to sneeze and was in need of her handkerchief, and her sneeze coincided with the pop. But she had seen nothing with the hankie against her eyes. When she did look, her companion had fallen on the floor and was no more.

De Gier squatted next to the corpse. The light-brown skin, the aquiline nose, the noble, dark eyes.

"This Arab," de Gier said, standing again, looking down on the lady, "was your friend?"

Her long eyelashes fluttered. "A mere acquaintance."

"A citizen of what country?"

"Persia?"

"You aren't sure?"

Her lovely neck turned first left then right.

"Your name?"

She did know her name. "Everts. Mrs. Everts. Call me Yvette."

Adjutant Grijpstra had enough. His heavy hand rested on the maitre's shoulder. "Everybody out now. Tell your guests and waiters to leave."

"Is he unwell?" patrons were asking, nudging each other. "Why is he bleeding?"

"He's dead," the waiters were answering. They knew what was what.

"Make sure they pay first," the maitre whispered fiercely, addressing the staff. Then he apologized loudly to the guests for the inconvenience.

The waiters carried in coats. "Me, too?" Mrs. Everts asked, getting up.

"No," Grijpstra said crossly. De Gier flicked his lighter. The lady had a cigarette between her fingers and needed a light.

The detectives were quiet. They admired plaster-of-paris angels, full size, sculptured in the domed ceiling, forever raising trumpets, forever not playing a note. Yvette was quiet, too. Then:

"His name was Omar, I think," she said.

"Really," Grijpstra said, smiling. "He takes you out? You're not sure of his name?"

"Did you meet in the street?" de Gier asked. "He whistled? You stopped?"

Mrs. Everts smiled forgivingly. "No. The agency rented me to him. I'm a hostess with an escort service. A man pays and he's got my company for the evening."

"And the night?" de Gier asked.

"And the night."

Grijpstra looked away. He was lighting a cigar. He said, "Bah" to the cigar.

"I disappoint you?" Yvette asked. "You're not aware of the hard facts of life? A woman has to make a living."

"Yak," de Gier said, looking at the adjutant's cigar. "You should change your brand."

"A whore and her pickup," Yvette said softly.

"Paid company," de Gier said. "It's all in the day's work. We can take it, Mrs. Everts." He pointed at the corpse. "But he couldn't, it seems. He fell into hell. If you're a moll, would the bad man be a gangster?"

"I didn't know him," the lady whispered. "He seemed well educated. A businessman. Im- and export, perhaps?"

"Sergeant," Grijpstra said gruffly, "don't jump to conclusions." He addressed the lady. "Don't mind him, Miss. We had a hard day." He held up a finger. "Picked up a dead junkie from a houseboat." He held up another finger. "Found an old man three weeks dead in this bed. The neighbors called us. Now this. The sergeant is still young. Maybe he should be in traffic."

Yvette smiled at the sergeant. "It's all right. I like you, anyway."

De Gier went off to phone. When he came back he said, "They'll be here in a minute. Photographers. A doctor. You didn't shoot him, ma'am?"

"Call me Yvette," the lady said. "These are modern times and we're about the same age. No, I didn't shoot him."

"Can I look in your bag?"

She passed the bag. "I'd rather you didn't."

De Gier's fingers prodded and came up with an object.

"No," Yvette said, "put it back, that's mine. It's needed, I don't want it confiscated."

The sergeant deposited the square heavy wallet in Grijpstra's hands. Grijpstra opened the leather flap. "This is not a wallet, Mrs. Everts, it's a clever hideout for a deadly weapon." He took out the tiny gun. "A Derringer. Small but efficient. Shoots magnum point twenty-two's. If they hit, they kill. Doesn't matter much where they hit."

"It takes two bullets," Yvette said. "They're both there."

Grijpstra opened the gun. "So they are. So they are. Never used it, did you now. Why do you need the weapon, Mrs. Everts?"

"Well," Yvette said. "That's rather a silly question. Aren't I in a risky position while I ply my trade? The agency does attempt to screen the clients, but once in a while I do meet a crazy fellow who likes to play odd games. Then it's nice to know I can defend myself. Or I'm pushed out of a car because I've changed my mind. I don't want to go to the client's hotel room, after all. The man is too drunk or he insists that I share his dope. And once out in a cold dark street, I'm easy prey for muggers. The mugger wants my wallet. I take out the wallet. I kill him with my wallet."

"Have you killed any muggers lately?" de Gier asked.

Yvette smiled. "There could always be a first time."

"Yes," Grijpstra said. "You're under arrest. The charge is carrying an unlicensed firearm. You will be aware that the penalty is severe."

"Never," Yvette said. "Not for me. I'm a welfare mother. You won't put me in jail out of concern for my child. He expects me to come home and make him breakfast. Your superiors won't support the charge."

"Another charge?" de Gier said. "Drawing welfare is illegal if you have other income. So you haven't declared your income as an escort hostess."

"You haven't been reading the papers," Yvette said. "Charges against welfare mothers are usually dropped. Stop threatening me."

The body was photographed. The doctor took a look.

"Yes?" Grijpstra asked.

"Yes," the doctor said. "Have a nice evening. Bye, now. Toodle-oo."

"Am I still under arrest?" Yvette asked. "The cab drivers are on strike. I can't get out of here." She stretched a long leg. "Not on these high heels."

"Omar drove you here?" Grijpstra asked.

She nodded. "In a rented Mercedes. The car is outside. He was staying at the Hilton. You really plan to lock me up?"

Grijpstra looked at de Gier. "Take care of her. I'll have a look at the car. See you later at the station."

The adjutant stalked off. De Gier offered his arm to the lady. An ambulance driver and his mate dumped the body on a stretcher.

"Why are you driving a wreck?" Yvette asked, sliding into the detectives' ancient VW. "A rustbucket, about to fall apart."

"Beauty is skin-deep," de Gier said. "A faithful soul hides under unpolished dents. Where would you like to go?"

"I thought you were taking me to jail?"

"I thought you have a child at home?" The engine whined to life. "How old is your son?"

"Martin just turned ten. He shouldn't know about this. I live in Luyken Street." She watched the window wipers. "Now it's raining, too."

De Gier found the street. "Number?"

She gave it. "Want to come in for a moment"

De Gier drove on, looking for a place to park.

"I should have brought my coat," she said. It was raining hard. The wipers had trouble keeping the windscreen clean. "Now I have to slop through puddles. I only bought these shoes today."

De Gier had found a place. "You won't get wet. I'llcarry you across the puddles."

He found a rolled-up coat on the back seat. "We're well equipped."

He held up the coat. "See? It even has a hood."

Yvette slipped into the coat. De Gier got out and waited for her on the sidewalk. He bent his knees, put one arm across her soulders and another under her knees, and swooped her up easily.

"Comfortable?"

She giggled from the black depth of the hood. "Oh, yes. You're my hero. I didn't know there were any left. Are you truly a hero?"

"I am," de Gier said. "Quaking in my boots, I fight for fun. I usually lose but I don't care. Perpetual failure is good character training."

Her head rested against his shoulder. "You waste energy for free?"

He peered into the hood after jumping a puddle. "I do get my wages." He didn't make the next jump as perfectly as planned. "But rewards tend to spoil the game. I accept neither medals nor promotion." He laughed softly. "The cause is lost, the future dim, but aren't we having a good time while we muddle about?"

"That's nice," Yvette said. "When you laugh, your chest rumbles. You have an immense chest. I like it here. Why don't you carry me around the block?"

More water splashed into de Gier's shoes as he carefully put her down. She opened a door that led to a long steep staircase. She looked around. "I'll go first. Promise not to look under my skirt."

There was a landing upstairs and another door, recently and neatly painted, with her name calligraphed in slanting lettering above a shiny antique brass knocker.

Yvette coughed as she reached for the key and fitted it into the lock. "The climb always wears me out." The door swung open. "Step into my nest, handsome sergeant."

De Gier looked around at the Seventeenth Century rosewood set of drawers, a mahogany bookcase, fresh flowers artfully arranged in alabaster vases. "Luxury!" A small boy was watching TV. He got up to shake the visitor's hand.

"Martin," Yvette told de Gier.

"Rinus," de Gier said. "Pleased to meet you. Martin. I had to take your mother home. Bad weather."

Martin kissed his mother. "Where is Omar, Mom? Did something go wrong?"

Yvette stroked his hair. "Omar had to go back to his country. Anything good on television?"

"No. The news was bad again. Black people dying and an airplane fell down. In the snow somewhere. You could see the broken wings and they say all the people are dead."

"Never watch the news," de Gier said. "I haven't got a TV. It's nice not to know."

"I'll get him a VCR," Yvette said, "with cartoons or something. He doesn't need a social conscience, that's only weight."

"How about a tank full of goldfish?" de Gier suggested. "They're fun to watch." He shook his head. "No. Goldfish feel caught, too. Maybe he should just watch the sky."

"I'll go to bed," Martin said. They wished him good night. He shook de Gier's hand again. "Nice to meet you Rinus. Are you Mom's friend?"

"Yes," de Gier said. "No babysit?" he asked, when the door closed.

Yvette checked her watch. "She'll be here in half an hour. Maybe I can still catch her at home. Will that be okay? For me to use the phone?"

"Why not?" de Gier asked, admiring framed prints signed by a known artist. His finger traced the backs of textbooks on a shelf.

Yvette phoned, then turned to de Gier. "Didn't you say I was under arrest? I thought maybe suspects aren't allowed to make phonecalls."

"You're a student?" asked de Gier.

"Yes. I'm almost done. I'll be a lawyer. Care for a drink?"

The bar, hidden in the rosewood cupboard, was well stocked. "Don't you think I'm good? I never graduated from high school, I married stupidly—we both worked in factories for years—then I woke up at last. I'm intelligent. I went back to school and passed all the evening courses. Then I became an escort lady and go to university days. Another few months and I'll have my degree."

De Gier caressed his mustache. "Your husband?"

"He didn't like it. We divorced."

"He doesn't support you?"

She shrugged. "Should he? He needs his money. He married again, he's got new kids and all. I take care of myself."

"And Martin?"

"He sometimes visits his father. I don't mind." She held up a glass.

"What will it be, sergeant?"

"Soda, please. I'm working now."

She poured from a chilled can.

"Welfare and the agency," de Gier said. "You're doing well. Why did you say you had only just met Omar?"

She poured a stiff whiskey and gulped it down. "I didn't want to get involved. Omar was my special client. The agency is tough. They insist on being paid even if the relationship becomes more personal. Omar paid them and tipped me. He wallowed in money. He sold Persian oil. I've known him for some months."

"I might not have found out," de Gier said. "Why did you ask me in?"

She smiled. "I'm a weak woman. I liked the way you held me."

"You keep lying," de Gier said. "That's okay. All suspects lie. Now, did you see the killer?"

Yvette flopped down on the couch. "Don't be so serious, Sergeant. I saw the man. He squints. He's a Persian, too, I think. The waiter's description was accurate enough. It was all over in a moment. The man seemed to want to pass our table, then stopped and shot Omar. There was something on the gun—a silencer, I suppose."

"Can I phone?" de Gier asked.

"Yes," Grijpstra said. "I checked with the car-rental people and I phoned the hotel. Omar Sarab is the name. He's in the morgue now and I went through his pockets. There was a business letter from the Berg and Company oil firm in Rotterdam. I rose Mr. Berg at his home. My news hardly surprised him. Omar was corrupt, sold oil cheaply if Berg came up with some cash on the side. Lots of cash, I presume. Maybe ten thousand dollars on every deal. Omar couldn't take the money home so he spent it here. Some of it on the lady?"

"Have you ever read the Koran?" de Gier asked.

"What does it say?"

"It describes sobriety," de Gier said. "The simple life here and the good life later in heaven. Persia is run by a priest. The priest is tough."

"He had Omar shot?"

"Just a guess," de Gier said.

"My guess, too," Grijpstra said. "A political murder. Out there religion is political. That leaves us out, Sergeant. I'll type a note to the Secret Service. They can file it. The killer must be on his way out already."

"Not yet, Adjutant. There are no planes at this time of night."

"The case is closed, Sergeant."

"Wait," de Gier said. "I've really read the Koran. It also prescribes hospitality. Hospitality is one of our own virtues, too. Here is a foreigner having dinner in our city and he gets shot. We failed to protect him. I say we do some work."

"Please, Sergeant." Grijpstra sighed. "Admire a job well done. No mess. No innocent parties were hurt. Come here and sign my report. Then we're done, you hear?"

"Sure," de Gier said. "Another virtue is friendship. You're my friend. Just a little project to share. It will only take a couple of short hours. I'll pick you up at the Apollo Boulevard, I have an idea."

"How can I go anywhere if you have the car?"

"Take the streetcar," de Gier said. "A Number Twenty-four. It goes every few minutes. Get off at Beethoven Street and I'll be right along." He put down the phone.

Yvette's hand rested lightly on the sergeant's sleeve. "Stay out of this, Rinus. Omar knew he was taking risks. Moslems live by their weapons. Your adjutant doesn't want to go. He's right. Phone him back and spend some time with me."

De Gier hesitated. She kissed his chin.

"No," de Gier said.

She pushed his chest with both hands. "Such a perfect knight, wasting time and energy on the wrong cause. Be a true hero. I can help. Travel all over and bags of gold to spend, and when you're here you can be with me."

"I really have to go now," de Gier said.

"You're free, you know," Yvette said. "Think about it. You can do what you like."

Adjutant Grijpstra was wet through, his glistening face only partly protected by his threadbare overcoat's collar. "What happened to you?"

"Unexpected trouble," de Gier said. "I saw a van opening its sliding doors, with hands that came out. Bicycle-thieving hands."

"We're the murder brigade," Grijpstra reminded him. "Will you ever learn minding our business?"

"I thought it would only take a minute." De Gier grinned. "But they were fighting types. I got them down after a bit, but then the patrol car was late."

"Busybody." Grijpstra frowned. "And me getting soaked here. Now what do we do? Can I please go home?"

"See here," de Gier said. "Our hitman, properly motivated, was sent by a high priest, but murder upsets the staunchest of spirits. I theorize that our suspect was shaken. Now what does a shaken Persian do while he waits for the morning and the plane that'll fly him home? Wouldn't he be looking for some comfort? Where would he find that?"

"We're not visiting brothels tonight," Grijpstra said. "I absolutely refuse. Catch your own wild goose."

"He's a devout Moslem, Adjutant, averse to women and wine. I believe he's with his own kind, right this minute. There aren't too many Persians about in Amsterdam, and the few who bless us with their presence gather in a cafe."

"Where?"

De Gier pointed. "In that side street."

"Hmm."

"Am I right?"

"You could be," Grijpstra said. "You've been right before. Light-tan trousers? Brown-leather jacket? Dark? Shaven hair?"

"He squints," de Gier said.

"Ah," Grijpstra grumbled. "So the lady did see him." His wet hand patted de Gier's arm. "Rinus, listen. That cafe will be full of automatics. They may have bazookas. You want to attack with two puny pistols? That's against instructions. We should phone for assistance."

"And not get it," de Gier said. "It takes hours before a SWAT team can get together. What does our very own commissaris say? In a case like this we can never be too fast. The killer is still nervous—he's bound to make mistakes."

Grijpstra dropped his soggy cigar. "Let's go."

De Gier parked the Volkswagen. The cafe's windows had been covered with sheets of brown paper.

"Not a welcoming place, Sergeant."

"A nasty place," de Gier agreed. "I went in once. They serve goat's leg with the hair still on. The waiters keep rushing away to pray. The Ayatollah watches from the wall."

"Closed!" an unshaven old man shouted. "Go home—this place private!" Grijpstra showed his identification. "Police. Checking your residence permits. And a good evening to you."

The café was crowded. The clients, bearded and fierce-eyed, snarled and gestured. A young man answering the waiter's and Yvette's description slipped through a door to the back.

De Gier ran after him and cornered him in a back room. The suspect reached for his gun—too late, for the sergeant's fist had already hit his jaw. He stumbled. The sergeant shoved and the suspect fell. De Gier knelt on his chest and pulled the pistol from his armpit. "Let's go," de Gier said, getting to his feet and dragging the young man up with him.

In the cafe, the Persians came forward, shoulder to shoulder.

"Police!" Grijpstra shouted, walking backward to the door. "No trouble. Keep quiet. Back to your coffee, have a good time!"

The suspect was pushed onto the Volkswagen's rear seat. De Gier sat next to him. Grijpstra drove the car away from the sidewalk, drying his face with a dirty handkerchief. "I tell you, everyone in there was armed. Must I really work with you? You'll be the death of me, Sergeant."

De Gier showed Grijpstra the young man's gun. "Proof, Adjutant. We have our man."

"Hurrah," Grijpstra said. "Back to the station. Lock suspect up. Close for the day. I'll buy you a drink."

"How come I always pay?" de Gier asked. "Your invitations are too costly."

Suspect mumbled in Persian.

"English?" de Gier asked.

Suspect mumbled in English. About Duty Done. Things had gone well. Allah was with him. What happened to him now wouldn't matter to him. The folks back home would be proud of him. "Kill me," suspect mumbled. "I'll go to heaven."

"Not yet," de Gier said. "The houris will have to wait a while."

"What are houris?" Grijpstra asked.

"Moslem angels that'll make love to him. Call girls upstairs. — You're better off here," de Gier said to the suspect. "You'll have a rest."

"One idealist catches another," Grijpstra said. "You should let him go, Sergeant. He's your brother in the spirit."

"Let's interrogate him first."

"You think he'll talk?"

"Of course," de Gier said. "His courage is like mine. It evaporates under stress. He'll sing like an egret."

"What's an egret?"

"A Persian bird."

In the detective's office, the suspect sat straight on the edge of his chair, with his arms crossed defensively. "He won't say anything," Grijpstra complained, "and I'm running out of time. Can we go and have that drink now?"

"Allow me," de Gier said. He took a pair of new gloves from a drawer. He put them on slowly, staring at the suspect.

"Now what?" Grijpstra asked.

"These gloves are a birthday present from my sister," de Gier said. "I never thought I'd have a use for them, but the suspect now thinks I'm going to beat him up."

Grijpstra studied the suspect's face. "I'll help you. He lit a fat cigar, sucking furiously so that the tip glowed a sinister red.

"Please," the suspect said. "Don't."

"Name of your boss?" the sergeant snarled. The leather of his gloves creaked. Grijpstra's cigar sparked.

"Karim."

"Address?"

"Rubens Street." Suspect also supplied the number. Grijpstra put down his cigar. De Gier took off his gloves. "Doesn't ignorance help? They should instruct their killers better. Don't they know we're the most tolerant cops on earth?" He picked up the phone. "One suspect for the cellblock."

Two uniformed constables came to fetch the killer. "Frisk him," Grijpstra said. His lighter is a bomb, the clasp of his belt a knife. He's probably hiding poison, too."

"Now," Grijpstra said in the Volkswagen, "this is far as I go. Mr. Karim will have diplomatic status. He'll also be armed, employ bodyguards, and keep dogs. The apartment will be guarded by electronic gadgets. A leopard will jump us when we ring the bell."

"Just one last move," the sergeant said gently. "If there are any complaints, we'll listen to them tomorrow. Today is still today. It'll be nice, Adjutant, a chase in the dark. A challenge, I daresay. Jane lives in the Rubens Street. I'll go through her apartment and attack from the roof."

"Leave Jane out of this," Grijpstra said. "Jane is a street cop, not an assassin like you. That she seems to like you is no reason to risk her dear life."

"You ring the bell." De Gier said. "Kick the door. By now he's warned. He'll escape a via the roof. I'll wait for him and make the arrest."

"His finger will be on the trigger of an Uzi machine gun."

"Aimed at me, Adjutant. You'll be safe below."

"And what if he hits you?"

"You'll be rid of me."

"True, true," Grijpstra said. "Enough of this. I promise I'll pay for the drinks. Let's go. I know a nice bar that's still open."

"Rinus," Jane said, "are you out of your mind? Do you know what time it is? Ignore me at the station and visit me here whenever you like? Are you drunk? Are you crazy?"

"Sober," de Gier said. "Working."

Jane stepped back. "You really think I'm available whenever you feel a little hyper?"

"I am," de Gier said, "pursuing a dangerous criminal. I'm sorry I have to bother you, but I need to get on the roof. Let me get out through a window. Then go back to bed. I may be a while."

"I'll help."

"No," de Gier said. "It's blowing hard. You might be blown away."

De Gier stood on the windowsill with Jane holding onto his legs. He stretched and grabbed the gutter. His legs swung free. He crawled onto the roof, looked down at the street, and switched on his flashlight. The lights of the parked Volkswagen below blinked. De Gier slithered on wet roof-tiles, averting his face from the cold wind. Grijpstra got out of the car and rung Karim's bell. He stepped aside and waited.

There were clouds and no moon. De Gier stumbled about, ready to give in. Maybe political fanatics can stay cool. The Sergeant would give it another minute.

The wind howled but there were also other sounds. A squeaky trapdoor?

Karim hoisted his bulk onto the roof. His fear of heights made him dizzy. It's easy to slip on a wet roof. Where was he?

"Hello?" de Gier shouted.

Karim fired. The bullet whined through the night. Where had the voice come from?

"Drop your pistol!" de Gier shouted. "We have you surrounded! We're also waiting below! You're under arrest—surrender, sir!"

Karim cursed. De Gier cursed, too. They both fired in turn. De Gier missed on purpose. "Drop your gun!" I'm not really a hero, de Gier was thinking. All this frightens me. I hate heights. Here I am, a hundred feet up in a moving sky, confronted by a holy man with Allah on his side. What supports me, except my doubt?

"Mister Karim?"

Karim was portly and no longer young. His son had just been killed in a desert drenched by oil. His other son, a boy, was a prisoner of war. His daughters shuffled about wrapped up in black cloth, with their beautiful eyes, the eyes of their mother, peering innocently through slits. Karim prayed seven times to day. Now he was lost on a heathen roof.

"Yes?"

"Don't be foolish. Drop your gun. Raise your hands."

I've done the right thing, Karim thought. Omar was a traitor. He forgot the revolution. Omar sold his soul. Supreme justice killed him, I was merely a tool.

Karim fired again.

"Last chance!" de Gier shouted. "I'm counting to three. Then I'll be coming for you!"

No, please, Karim prayed. He kept firing until his gun clicked. He fumbled with the new clip. It slipped from his trembling hand. The shadow ahead crept closer. Karim stumbled, fell, tried to roll away. Had Allah come for him? Was he being lifted into heaven? Then why was he falling?

Grijpstra heard Karim's agonized yell rising feebly from the yard behind the apartment building. The adjutant sighed and returned to the car. He picked up the microphone attached to the dashboard.

It took long minutes before a patrol car arrived. De Gier was back in the street by then, standing next to Jane. His teeth chattered.

"Now what have you done?" Jane asked. "I knew that poor Arab. We bought flowers at the same stall. A nice, polite old man. I know his wife, too. I've often helped her with her shopping."

"I'm sorry," de Gier said.

"Well, now," the commissaris said later the next day, "a job well done, I have to agree. Murders should be solved quickly or we lose the thread."

De Gier stared at his trembling hands. Grijpstra stirred his coffee.

"Not that I don't abhor violence," the commissaries said. "It shouldn't be necessary."

"He fell, sir," de Gier said.

"Yes. Quite. Now what about this Mrs. Everts? She's only mentioned in your report. No charges, Sergeant? Are we ignoring an unlicensed, nasty little gun and income that wasn't filed with our tax department? There'll be no action?"

De Gier tried to roll a cigarette. "Sir?" Grijpstra asked. "Should we waste our time? The court doesn't welcome that sort of thing. A welfare mother with a child?"

"A future lawyer," the commissaries said. "Do we need lawyers like that?"

"And the gun,". Grijpstra a said. "Just a toy in a way. In her present profession, she does need protection. We no longer do a good job. There are muggings galore."

"The citizens arming themselves?" the commissaris asked. He pushed the report away. "Very well. Take a few days off. Take a rest. See you next week." He rubbed his leg.

"How's your rheumatism, sir?"

The commissaries looked at the rain beating against the window. He nodded. "I'll feel better in the spring."

Yvette phoned. "Am I under arrest or not?"

"Not," Grijpstra said.

"And my Derringer?"

De Gier took the phone. "Will you be home tonight?"

"I'm working."

"Tomorrow?"

"Tomorrow night, too."

"I can't think that far ahead." De Gier put the phone down.

She arrived during the weekend, after telephoning him first. The hairdresser had readjusted her hair modishly, adding just a touch of the latest punk style. Her mohair coat appeared brand new. De Gier helped her out of the coat. She wore a paratrooper's suit underneath, dotted, camouflaged subtly. The ideal apparel for an independent spirit. She paused in de Gier's door, taking in the apartment.

"You *live* here?"

"Sure. You don't like my home?"

"But it's so *small*."

"It's only for me," de Gier said. "And Tabriz." He picked up the cat. The cat was fat, bald in spots, low on its legs.

"Charming," Yvette said. "I trust she's well tempered."

"Not really." He put the cat down. Tabriz mumbled to herself, rowing her legs. She shot off to the kitchen. De Gier pointed at the bed, held up by a polished copper frame. "Don't mind its appearance. It's old, but it'll hold you in comfort. I have no chairs.—A cup of tea? I've got some made."

He passed her a cup and the Derringer that he retrieved from a drawer. She opened her bag and dropped the weapon into its welcoming slit. The bag snapped shut. "Thanks."

De Gier bowed. "My pleasure. I oiled it for you. The hinge was quite rusty."

Yvette crossed her long legs. "You live in a cubbyhole. I'm surprised at you, Sergeant, a man of your status. What's that growing on your balcony? Some rare plants?"

"Weeds," de Gier said. "Dug up from a wasteland. I like weeds. They grow flowers in summer and the birds come and pick the seeds this time of the year. Sparrows mostly. They hang upside down when they eat."

Yvette waited for him to light her cigarette. "Birds and plants? Sparrows and weeds? You could have peacocks and palm trees. Wouldn't you like that better?"

De Gier thought. "Yes. Why not?"

"You can have all you can imagine." Yvette's hand touched his hair. "That's why I came, to share that truth. The agency is opening up connections from the Middle East through here to the Caribbean Islands. You could live on Aruba, in a villa of your own. The agency needs heroes like you, who will travel."

De Gier looked up. "You're qualified. Why give me the job?"

Yvette pushed out a moist lower lip. "The agency prefers a man. Besides, there's Martin. He needs another six years of care."

"No," de Gier said. "My quest is different, there's no room for greed."

She jumped off the bed and paced the apartment, looking at the books. "You read."

"Sometimes."

She picked up a volume. "In French?"

"Yes," de Gier said. "My French is weak, but it's nice to guess at words, give them my own meaning"

"I like crime novels."

De Gier grinned. "Prefer your own field?"

She shrugged. "But they are nonsense, too. Good versus bad. Good always wins. It doesn't. You know that."

He shrugged, too. "We can try."

She knelt next to him and pushed his shoulder. "Don't tell me you believe in silly morals. Why did you push Karim off that roof? You defined him as bad? What had he done to you?"

De Gier kept grinning. "He wouldn't let Omar have dinner in peace. I'm a cop, I protect the good manners of my city."

"You're hopeless," she said. "Maybe I should take you for what you are. I've slept with idiots before—maybe there are all kinds."

"I bet there are," de Gier told her. "Allow me to help you into your coat."

She smiled at him from the door. "Goodbye."

"Bye now," de Gier said. "Say hello to Martin.'

Ellery Queen's Mystery Magazine, 1986

Off Season

It was off-season at the monastery where I was, as they say, studying Zen Buddhism. It seemed to me that I wasn't studying anything. My legs hurt when I sat in meditation and my meditation consisted of a blurred mixture of a lot of thoughts. They told me I had to get rid of the thoughts but there were so many of them, like ants crawling, millions of ants, most of them voracious, and they were hard to fight. I could crush a few now and then but they were always replaced. And now the training season had stopped and most of the monks had wandered off. The teacher had gone too and I asked for permission to go.

"Will you be back?" the head monk asked.

"Sure."

"When?"

"In a month."

He bowed and poured tea. I bowed. We drank tea. We bowed again. I left within an hour. I had an old American motorcycle and stuffed the saddlebags with clothes and a sleeping bag. A map was stuck on the tank, in a plastic cover. I had no idea where I was going but it is always nice to have a map. The map was Japanese and I could only read a few of the characters which indicated the place names. The trip was a dream and I was guided by mysterious hieroglyphs. I felt I was well prepared.

I planned to go west, and then north and to stick to country roads. I didn't hurry, stopping at roadside restaurants to eat noodles and fish-soup, and I slept in a small army tent next to the motorcycle. It rained for a few days and I accepted a farmer's invitation to stay in his house. We met in an eating place. He had greeted me and I said something in Japanese and we got involved in something which sounded remarkably like a conversation. I didn't have too many words and he spoke the local dialect, but we smiled and bowed too, and shared a small bottle of sake.

His house was close to a village and I went shopping the next day. The one-legged American was shopping too. We said "good morning" to each other and continued our shopping but I had had time to look at him. He must have been close to fifty years old and he had shaved his large skull which shone and had a nutbrown color. Evidently he spent a lot of time outside. He walked on crutches, managing to hold on to a satchel which contained the vegetables he had just bought. He chatted with the shopkeeper who seemed to know him well, bent down to talk to a child and everybody around greeted him. We met again a few minutes later, I was starting my motorcycle but my vigorous kicking drew little response; the engine kept on stalling.

"Trouble?" he asked

"She is slow," I said, "but she will come to life if I persist."

"Carburetor," he said. "These old Harleys have funny carburetors. There's a float in them, like in a flush toilet, and some dirt may stop the float. Then the engine floods. It's happening now. See?"

He pointed at a trickle of gas, oozing down the side of carburetor.

"Yes," I said, "I don't know anything about technical things. I'll have it repaired."

"I'll do it," he said, shifting the position of his crutches and looking at the engine again. "I live over there, that small house in the field beyond the pines trees. Get her started and ride her down there. We can have lunch. Where are you from? England?"

"Holland," I said.

He thought for a while and then nodded gravely, acknowledging the existence of my country.

The door of the small house was open and I unzipped my boots and climbed on the verandah. I cold hear him moving about the house, clattering with pots.

"Come in," he said, "fried fish today. We call'em suckers in the States. Fresh water fish with big mouths. They are good if they are fresh. And I have some fried eggplant, and pickles, and rice. Will that do?"

It sounded very good to me. At the monastery we ate boiled cabbage and a hot mixture of a lot of barley and a little rice. Plain fare. This sounded like a feast, but I had been eating well the last few days too, fried noodles and fancy pickles at the roadside restaurants and even some bread which I had baked in the farmer's oven.

The house was very clean and empty. The only objects around were for immediate use. A thin mattress, clothes, kitchen utensils, garden tools. "My workshop is outside," he said.

"I repair trucks mostly, and small tractors. The farmers bring them to me."

"Is that what you do for a living?" I asked.

He shook his head. "No. I don't charge. They pay for the parts. I have a pension." He pointed at the non-existent leg.

"Lost it at Okinawa; they remember in the States and send me a check every month."

He had opened two big bottles of beer and we raised the glasses and drank. I thanked him for the food.

"That's all right. You can stay the night. I'll repair your motorcycle in the morning. It's too late now. Why are you in Japan?"

I told him about my stay in the monastery. I had stayed a year, I said, and would stay another year, maybe longer.

"Why are you there?" He asked

"To become enlightened."

He laughed, slapping his thigh and wiping tears out of his eyes. He laughed for a long time. A full minute maybe. Finally he stopped.

"I am sorry," he said.

I was hurt but not too badly. I was getting used to being laughed at. The monks would come out in the garden if they saw me pissing against a tree and they would hang on to each other helplessly as I watered way. "Just like a horse," they would say and begin to laugh again. I amused them in other ways too. They couldn't understand that my kegs hurt me when I had to sit in the meditation hall, and they would smile if I hobbled around, one leg lame because of bad blood circulation.

We had more beer and went out on the verandah. The house was built on a low hill and we had a good view of the countryside. I saw groves of pinetrees and the roofs of thatched farms, a four-storied pagoda enthroned on the next hill. The sound of wooden clappers and a bell drifted down to us.

"That's the old man," my host said; "he is all by himself up there. In the evening he sits for an hour and he always gives the proper signals. One clap four bells when he starts, one bell two claps when he stops."

"Like in the monastery," I said.

"Yes. The old man is of the same faith."

"Faith?" I asked

"Whatever you like," he said slowly. "I was giving it a name. It has no name."

"Do you know the old man up there?" I asked.

"He is my teacher."

He went in and came back with six bottles. They were big bottles and I braced myself. I would get drunk. I didn't mind getting drunk but it wouldn't hurt to be prepared.

"So how long have you been here?" I asked.

He spoke for some time. He had come with the Marines and he had been fighting for four days when he lost his leg and was taken back to a ship, and later to the States. "I killed a lot of soldiers before the leg came off. A hundred maybe. I shot them with a machine gun, they came rushing at us and I just kept on killing them. There was a heap of corpses and they were crawling over it and I went on shooting."

I mumbled something. I was too young for the war and didn't know what he was talking about. I had killed a rat once, with a poker, and I killed her babies too. The rat was in the garage of my father's house. I had been thinking of the rat and her offspring lately, when I was supposed to meditate.

"But why did you come back?"

"I kept on dreaming about the dead Japanese soldiers," he said, "and then I was seeing them when I was awake too. I saw them crawling over their own corpses and I was shooting them. I saw a psychiatrist bt it didn't help much. After a year's treatment I was still seeing them. Then I came back. I wandered around for a while and settled here. Ten years ago."

"You must like it here."

"Yes," he said, filling my glass. "I repair their machines now, it's more constructive."

"And you still see the dead soldiers?"

"Sometimes."

The sun was setting behind the pagoda. It was the time of the evening that everything suddenly becomes very exact. The branches of the trees were outlined sharply against the pale soft sky and the pagoda looked as if it had been cut out of the cloud which sat behind it, its edges lit up dark orange.

I pointed at the temple.

"And he lives there? Your teacher?"

"Yes. He is a priest."

"A master? A Zen master?"

He shrugged. "I don't know what Zen means and I have never asked him if he is a master. He is very old. Eighty I think. I met him in the village, I had been here a year so and I was learning the language. It goes quickly if you hear nothing else. You are the first gaijin I have seen in years, the tourist buses miss this place."

"What did he say?"

"He told me to come and see him. I did, the same afternoon. He taught me to sit in meditation and told me to sit for two hours every day. I had to get up at two and stop at four. Then I had to go and see him."

"He ordered you to do that?"

He inclined his head, and his skull gleamed. "Yes. He knew why I had come. I have been going to see him most days since then. Not tomorrow, that's why I can drink now. I like to drink but I can't go to see him with a smell on my breath and a headache."

"Have you ever tried?"

"No."

"Did he give you a koan?"

He nodded but I didn't ask him what koan. It's bad manners to discuss koans. My own teacher had told me so. In the monastery I saw him every morning and every evening. I had been given a koan too but I didn't understand it. I didn't even understand what the question was supposed to be and nobody wanted to explain it to me. I had to find out for myself.

I wanted to ask him if he had passed his koan but thought I shouldn't.

"I haven't passed my koan," he said a little while later, "but I have been going to see him nine years, most days. Usually he is asleep when I bow to him, he is old and not in the best of health. I used to shake him to wake him up and he would look at me and say 'what what?' and ring his bell. When he rings his bell I have to leave. Now I don't wake him anymore. I just go in, bow, wait a minute, and leave."

"Shit," I said.

"Pardon?"

"Shit," I said.

He laughed, "Yes sounds pretty silly, eh? Not to me though. He is there when I go to see him, that's enough. I don't want too many things anymore. I repair machines and the farmers bring me vegetables, and rice and sometimes a little meat. I found a way of chopping my own wood and I have a motorized tricycle which will take a quarter of a cord of firewood so I can go and get it myself. Sometimes I don't even touch my check. I paid for the repair of the pagoda last year. Just the materials. The labor was supplied by the people around here."

"Does your teacher have other disciples?"

"No, just me. He is retired. There's a monastery with a younger teacher close by. He has half a dozen lay disciples; I have met him but he is not for me. I am the old man's son now."

"But he is asleep," I said, and drank a little more beer. I would have to be careful, the house was beginning to sway and I still had to get my sleeping bag off the motorcycle. He made a gesture, sweeping my protest aside.

"In San Francisco my mother had a little pagoda," he said, slurring his words somewhat. "It was made of ivory and had four stories just like the one up there. The first story had a tiny door. I would open that door and peer inside but there was nothing inside. It used to sadden me. The pagoda was so beautiful, it had a spire pointing at the sky and small narrow verandahs encircling it. It pointed somewhere but it was empty. That pagoda over there is not empty."

"But he is asleep," I said stubbornly. "He doesn't know you have come to see him. You have sat for two hours and something has happened inside you. You have come to tell him about it but he doesn't know."

"Silence is a good answer," my host said.

I put my glass down. There were still some bottles around but I had had enough. I got my sleeping bag. He had cleared up by the time I came back and gave me a hard little pillow. "How do you go there?" I asked before I fell asleep.

"I walk."

"The path is steep, it must be half a mile or more. And you only have one leg."

A hand came up from under his padded blanket and touched my shoulder.

He was chuckling.

Parabola, 1976

Inspector Saito and the Twenty-Sen Stamp

If, Saito thought, I really am as intelligent as the police academy teachers unanimously stated at graduation, what am I doing in this impossible little room? There's snow on the ground and the park of the former Imperial Palace is close by. I could be walking between graceful pine trees and ancient lovely buildings. No civilian will be committing a serious crime at this time of the morning. I'll wait for the water to boil, have tea, and be on my way.

He pulled the mini-hibachi, in which charcoal had once glowed but which now housed an electric element, carefully toward him, spooned green tea powder into a cracked cup, poured boiling water from the kettle atop the hibachi, and made the tea foam by stirring it energetically with an old chopstick.

Someone knocked at the door. "Yes?"

Kobori marched in, stopped, and bowed. "Morning, Inspector-san."

Saito sighed and pushed the cup to the edge of his desk. "Morning, Sergeant. Here you are. I thought you had night duty."

Kobori lowered himself carefully on a chair after placing his cap, visor forward, under its tatty straw seat. He picked up the cup with both hands and watched the Inspector over its edge. "Yes, Saito-san, I should be home by now but I thought I'd better report in first."

Saito's mood improved. Kobori's antique good manners were comical and heartwarming. He opened a drawer of his desk, found a second cup, and once again busied himself with the tea ceremony. Kobori's uniform, in spite of a long night's work, looked as if it had just been torn out of a dry cleaner's plastic cover. He waited until Saito had taken his first sip.

"Inspector-san, there was a fire in the Kitayama Quarter. An old man, a Mr. Nogi, suffocated. I have submitted my report and thought that the matter had been taken care of, but a certain aspect still bothers me."

Saito nodded. "Let's have it."

Kobori cleared his throat. "It was like this. The fire wasn't exactly spectacular and the firemen took care of it in no time, but Mr. Nogi died all the same. He was home by himself. His housekeeper, Setsuko, was out for a walk. Nogi was admiring his stamp collection in the upstairs room and was probably drunk—we found an empty saki bottle under his table. The wastepaper basket behind him caught fire and the flames ignited the doormats. It may be that Nogi-san nodded off after he emptied his ashtray into the basket.

"He was rather a wasted little man, Saito-san—according to the housekeeper he suffered from stomach trouble. He was a retired petty official of the city's administration, seventy years old, and a lifelong bachelor."

"Who alerted the fire department?"

"A neighbor across the road, Mrs. Ichiyo, who wanted to admire the moonlight on the snow and saw flames licking at Mr. Nogi's upstairs window instead."

"And the housekeeper was out for a walk. What time did she come back?"

"At midnight. She had been out for an hour, to the gardens of the Daitokuji Temple, which is quite close. She said she couldn't sleep—and it was indeed a beautiful night."

"Out by herself?"

"Yes, Saito-san."

"An attractive woman?"

Kobori nodded. "Thirty years old. A provincial lady, from Hokkaido. They talk kind of strangely out there—I had some trouble catching what she said."

"Do you think Mr. Nogi was a wealthy man?"

"No. But not poor either. The house looked neat."

"Could his stamp album be worth money?"

"Perhaps. It was completely filled."

Saito lit a cigarette. "But it was still there. And the fire was caused by carelessness. But I take it you aren't sitting here to keep rne company. What haven't you told me, Sergeant?"

Kobori's sharply featured face inched forward and his deep-set eyes peered worriedly into Saito's. "That housekeeper was frightened and she didn't strike me as a nervous type. It can't have been my fault for

I hadn't been harassing her and the constable with me is a most peaceful man. The doctor immediately confirmed that Nogi had indeed been suffocated by smoke and had left with the corpse before she returned. I merely asked her the normal questions—whether the dead man had any relatives and if she intended to leave the house unattended—but she trembled and stuttered and it seemed that she could become aggressive any moment, like an animal that feels itself trapped. Interrogating her, I thought she might perhaps be in shock because her life had so suddenly changed—no more work, she was fond of the old man—but later, after leaving my report at the desk, I began to wonder about the whole thing."

"Do you know if there are any heirs?"

"A nephew who lives in Osaka." Kobori pulled a notebook from his side pocket and noted an address in tight square characters. He tore the page free and put it on Saito's desk. "Perhaps you could visit the woman today, if you have a minute, Inspector-san."

Chief Inspector Ikemiya waited at the open elevator door but Saito didn't move. Ikemiya gestured invitingly. "Aren't you getting out?"

"I forgot something," Saito mumbled and moved over to make space for his superior's ample body. The Chief Inspector looked at his assistant. "At it this early already? They told me at the desk that nothing happened last night."

"There was a fire," Saito said tonelessly.

The elevator stopped. "A fire?" said Ikemiya in the corridor. "Since when do we waste our time with fires?"

"A fire and a corpse."

"A burned corpse?"

"A choked corpse."

Ikemiya shook his head irritably. He grabbed Saito's arm. "You wouldn't have information that passed me by would you?"

"I don't know yet," Saito said. "Excuse me, this is my office. You'll hear from me, Ikemiya-san, if there is anything further to report."

Saito waited until Ikemiya's door banged shut at the end of the corridor before he picked up a book that had been wrapped in a piece of gold-embroidered silk and took it out of its cover. "Case 16B, now how did that go?" He found the chapter and read.

"When Yen Tsun was prefect of Yang-chou he once made an inspection journey through the district that had been entrusted to him. He suddenly heard someone shout out in fear rather than sadness. He had his chariot stopped and interrogated the person. She answered: 'My husband had an accident with fire and died.' Yen Tsun suspected her and ordered a constable to investigate the corpse. He saw that flies had gathered around the head and, looking closer, discovered the head of an iron nail that been hammered into the skull. It was proved that the woman, together with her paramour, had killed her husband and the suspects confessed."

Ikemiya entered without knocking and stood next to Saito. His fleshy hand hit the desk's edge. "No, Saito, not again! How often do I have to tell you that what happened in antique China has nothing to do with modern Japan?" He stared accusingly at his subordinate. "Times have changed, Inspector! We use computers today and know what happens on planets that the naked eye can hardly see. How can we learn anything from mouldy magistrates who had nothing to apply but their intuition and who utilized a whip to obtain confesions?"

Saito observed his chief quietly. Ikemiya produced a handkerchief and blew his nose. "This damned snow has given me a cold. Never mind, tell me what's wrong with your corpse. Do we have a case? And if so, do you plan working on it?"

Saito folded the book back into its silken wrap. "Sergeant Kobori thinks that the dead man's housekeeper behaved in an unusual manner and I was thinking I might go and see her."

"Tell me what you know."

Saito did.

Ikemiya extended a hand. "I've stopped smoking but this nonsense is too much. Give me a cigarette, Inspector." Saito did. Ikemiya inhaled deeply and blew out the smoke, coughing sharply. "Bah, a rich aristocrat like yourself who considers his work a hobby should allow himself a better brand. And what sort of a motive for this possible murder would you suggest?"

"I don't know yet."

Ikemiya regarded his glowing cigarette. "Nothing seems to be missing, you said. An emotional conflict? Nogi was a sickly old chap and Setsuko an attractive young woman. It has been ascertained that old lechers tend to abuse their servants, but a wench from Hokkaido isn't likely to be a pushover. Perhaps you should have a look at her. Spending an hour with her might be more enlightening than reading dusty books here."

He rubbed his stub in the ashtray. "But don't get carried away by youthful enthusiasm. We're here to keep things quiet, not to add to the confusion."

Saito let the car go and compared the address with Kobori's note. Except for a few sparrows arguing in the gutter nothing moved in the tiny street. The house seemed hardly damaged—only the paper in the upstairs window had been torn. Saito pushed the gate open and walked to the door that slid aside as soon as he had called good morning.

"Setsuko-san?" he said.

Her gaze was steady. "At your service."

Her simple kimono and starched apron did give her a rather provincial appearance. "I'm a police officer," Saito told her. "It's customary to check when there has been a deadly accident. Can I come in please?"

She guided him into the front room, arranged a cushion for him to sit on, and knelt opposite him on the worn mat. Her hands pulled at the hem of her apron. Saito smiled encouragingly. "I hear you have been working for Mr. Nogi for more than a year—is that right, Setsuko-san?"

"Yes."

"And you were a waitress in a restaurant before. Did Mr. Nogi meet you there?"

Her facial muscles hardened and she had trouble formulating her answer. "That's what I said." Her hand brushed impatiently across her face.

"How do you mean 'that's what I said'? Wasn't it true?"

Tears dribbled slowly toward her high cheekbones and her shoulders shook. "No."

"You didn't work in a restaurant?"

She swallowed and shot him a desperate look. "I shouldn't have said that. I knew, you would find out the truth."

"What truth?"

"That I used to be a photo model."

"A photo model," Saito said pensively. "And Mr. Nogi? How did you get to know your employer?"

"In the studio—behind the Raku Hotel."

Saito recalled the low-class hotel and the neighborhood behind it. Porno studios, rickety little wooden buildings where women allowed themselves to be photographed in any way the client specified for a small fee. "And you were ashamed to divulge that information to the policemen who came here last night?"

"Yes."

"I see. Mr. Nogi visited you often in the studio and offered you a job in the end. Is that correct?"

"Yes."

"So you weren't just a housekeeper?"

She pointed at the low ceiling. "We slept together, upstairs."

"You were paid?"

She nodded. "But I never managed to save. He only ate boiled rice and wouldn't let me cook for myself because the smell made him, hungry. To eat outside all the time costs a lot of money."

Saito produced a pack of cigarettes and offered them.

"No," she said. "It's unhealthy. Mr. Nogi smoked and the doctor said he shouldn't."

"Do you mind if I do?"

She got up and took a dish from a shelf. "Here," she said, "for your ashes."

"He drank too, didn't he?" Saito asked.

"No."

"No?"

She shut her eyes and nodded. "Yes, sometimes he did."

Saito sucked his cigarette thoughtfully. "Tell me—how did Nogi-san spend his time?"

Her apron strap had become undone and her hands trembled as she redid the knot. "He walked about the quarter and during the evenings he usually played with his stamps or we watched television."

Saito got to his feet. "May I see the upstairs room, Setsuko-san please?"

She led the way on the narrow staircase and he admired the seductive shape of her firm body, accentuated by the tight kimono. ("It was proved that the woman, together with her paramour, had killed her husband and the suspects confessed.")

She bowed awkwardly. "This is the room where Nogi-san died."

"Another question. You did lie to us before so please don't hold it against me if I am a little suspicious. Tell me, were you and Mr. Nogi married perhaps?"

She grinned nervously. "No, he didn't want to. I said we should get married so he wouldn't have to waste money on wages any more but he didn't want me to inherit the house. His nephew in Osaka has sons who are supposed to go to university later on. He said I should be able to take care of myself."

"That wasn't very nice of him, was it?"

"No."

"And what are your plans now, Setsuko-san?"

She bit her finger before she answered. "I don't know yet."

"You have no relatives?"

"No, nobody."

"No brothers, no sisters?"

"No one." She suddenly looked angry and he dropped his gaze. The room showed clear signs of the fire. A floor mat had changed into a mass of ashes and the table and rolled-up bedding in a corner were covered with yellowish flaky substance, remnants of the fire brigade's foam. He touched a saki bottle with the tip of his shoe.

"Mr. Nogi shouldn't have imbibed strong rice wine. Saki is pure poison for people who have stomach trouble."

She didn't comment. She had pressed herself against the wall. Her breathing was laborious and her fingers scratched on the material of her apron.

He bowed toward the table. "Here is the stamp album. Maybe I should take it with me." He shook a visiting card from his wallet, put it on the table, and picked up the album. "If Mr. Nogi's nephew should come you can tell him he can retrieve it at headquarters."

The woman still seemed stuck to the wall. Saito nodded pleasantly. "I'd better be on my way again. Goodbye, Setsuko-san. . ."

Chief Inspector Ikemiya frowned furiously. He had adjusted his revolving chair to its sharpest angle and kicked off his shoes. His feet rested on a stack of law books. Saito studied the energetic toes of his chief moving about gaily within the thin cotton of the fairly worn socks.

"You don't exactly obey your instructions," grumbled Ikemiya. "I thought I had asked you not to bother that woman unnecessarily. Why did she have to be arrested? The constables told me she didn't come easily. One of them had to go to emergency to have his face treated. Couldn't you have taken her in yourself?"

"That wouldn't have been a good move."

"No?" Ikemiya's heavy eyebrows wriggled sarcastically. "You weren't frightened of her, were you? I thought you were such a hero on the judo mat?"

Saito smiled politely. "I wasn't in uniform and I had made the mistake of sending the car away. If a man drags a handsome woman along the street passersby tend to interfere."

Ikemiya's big toe peeped through a fresh hole in his sock. Saito grinned. Ikemiya yanked his feet back.

"Saito," Ikemiya said, "this time you have gone too far. That woman is innocent. Haven't you see the pathologist's report? Alcohol in the blood and smoke in the lungs. That old codger was as drunk as a coot—whether you think the woman lied or not, he did choke on smoke. That balderdash you're trying to make me swallow, that case 16B taken out of context from a primeval manual on catching idiots is drivel. The 16B corpse had a nail in his noggin. Your corpse had breathed smoke. That scientifically proven fact tells us he wasn't killed before the fire occurred." Ikemiya's hairy fist hit the desktop. "There was *no* indication that violence was applied and confirmation that the housekeeper spoke the truth. So what do we do? We throw the lady in a cell." He held up a piece of paper. "Do you know what this is?"

"A letter?" Saito asked softly.

"Right—signed by Chief of Police Kato. The boss wants to know whether I truly think we have sufficient evidence to warrant the suspect's arrest. What do you suggest I should answer?"

"That we do have sufficient reason for suspicion," Saito said evenly. "I visited the lady across the street from the Nogi residence. Her name is Ichiyo. She stated that she knew Nogi well and often talked to him. She swore that Nogi hadn't enjoyed a drop of alcohol since he was operated on a year ago for bleeding in the stomach."

"Bah, that's what he told her. Alcoholics are professional liars."

"Mrs. Ichiyo also told me about the housekeeper's brother."

Ikemiya groaned and stuck out his hand. Saito filled it with a cigarette. Ikemiya pressed his silver desk-lighter. "Brother?" He inhaled deeply.

"Yes, Chief Inspector-san. Setsuko was alone in the world except for a brother who visited her regularly. Mr. Nogi was quite fond of the young man and told Mrs. Ichiyo he was intelligent and eager to learn."

"And *you* believe—"

"That the so-called brother was Setsuko's lover."

"And so, according to Case 16B, the loving couple did away with poor helpless Mr. Nogi." Ikemiya's fist banged on the armrest of his chair. "And why, if I may ask, Mr. Genius? To steal the gold bars carefully hidden by Nogi? Since when do retired minor officials dispose of secret wealth? Nothing was missing, was it? Even the stamp album had not been disturbed. You really want us to be shown up as nitwits? If the law is applied literally we can be accused of illegal harassing of a citizen."

Saito shook his head. "I don't think so, Ikemiya-san. The suspect has weakened her position considerably by telling lies."

The thin scarecrow surrounded by carelessly stacked boxes and stockbooks bowed to Saito. Saito greeted him, placed the album on the littered counter, and presented his card.

The storekeeper's mouth dropped open. "You are an inspector of the Criminal Investigation Department?"

Saito nodded. "We would value your advice. This collection interests us. It's an item involved in a serious case. Perhaps you could spare a few minutes to study its contents."

The dealer's thin lips curved into a sardonic grin. "You wouldn't be after a free appraisal, would you now, Mr. Official?"

"No," Saito said quietly. "Quite honestly, I don't know what I'm after, but you're an expert. All I can see is that the collection is complete. I'm hoping that what you say might give me some clues."

The storekeeper switched on a strong light and opened the album. I don't see a complete album very often. Either the owner is old or he is rich. The old stamps aren't printed any more and the modern stuff gets out of the machines by the millions and can be bought anywhere at any price. Here, the Nineteenth Century—that's what matters, you know."

Saito followed the spindly finger that caressed the page. "Ah," the dealer whispered almost reverently. "The 1874 series, with the imperial chrysanthemum as the chief decoration. The stamps of four, six, twenty, and thirty sen. The sen was worth something then and a hundred fitted into a yen. Now even a yen won't buy you a sliver of dried fish. May I take them out, Inspector-san?"

"Please."

The storekeeper opened a drawer and produced a pair of tweezers and a magnifier equipped with a focused light He switched the gadget on and pulled the twenty-sen stamp, an unsightly lilac-colored bit of irregularly notched paper, carefully from the album. "They come on thick paper and we're likely to pay a bit. And they come on thin paper, in which case we empty out the purse. On thin paper this darling is worth three and a half million, dear sir. And the collectors will pay that much too, for the series is harder to get all the time. Ah, just look at this!"

"It is a little torn." Saito was peering at what the dealer dangled in front of his eyes.

"You can see that without spectacles? You are a happy man." The dealer rummaged in his drawer again and came up with cut lenses attached to a small clasp. He clipped them onto his glasses "Right—let's take another peek."

The sudden flow of abuse was pronounced with such venom that Saito staggered away from the counter.

"Rubbish! Utter rubbish!" the dealer yelled. Torn and glued! Worthless junk! That's the way the fool who's after completeness crooks himself! What does he care as long as his album is full? The twenty-sen on thin paper, the rarity we all look for, it finally pops up and you're ready to thank the Goddess of Mercy, and it's damaged—you've still got nothing."

"Why don't you look further?" Saito asked. "So this one is bad—but there may be others."

"A pile of waste," the storekeeper said sadly. "Fool's gold." His eyes darted. "—Hey, what do we have here?" He pressed his magnifier on the other three stamps of the series and pulled on the goatee that pretended to hide his lack of chin. "Well, now, these seem to be in excellent order—they're on thick paper, of course, but even so they should be worth a couple of thousand." He moved the magnifier and scrutinized the rest of the page. "Here, very nice too, three thousand maybe. And here again, prime quality I would say." He turned the page and continued to nod approvingly. "First class. Not a bad collection after all." He took off his glasses and smiled at Saito. "Would you like a cup of tea, Inspector-san? This work always makes me thirsty. I go through half a gallon a day and my throat stays dry."

"You don't want to study the others?"

"Do you want me to? The new stuff is boring, I think. It's only the old ones that cheer me up. Here, I'll put those four back again before they get lost."

The dealer hooked his spectacles over his ears again and flipped back to the page where he had started. "Strange, don't you think?" he said. "Why would that one stamp, the only one that really matters, be in such a miserable condition? If it had been all right it would have been worth a hundred times more than all the rest of the collection together." He hesitated in the process of returning the first stamp to the album. "Huh."

"What is it?" Saito asked. "Do you see something?"

"The man wants to know if I see something." The dealer's complicated glasses nearly touched the page. "There must have been a protector here and it was ripped out with force. The marks are clear enough." The tip of his index finger rubbed the damaged paper. "You know what that is—a protector?"

"No."

"I'll explain it to you. See here—they come in strips of double clear plastic so the stamps can be inserted between the two layers. Once the stamp is in, you cut the strip with a pair of scissors so that you get a nice protector that fits the stamp exactly. There's glue on the back. You lick it and you press stamp and protector into the album." He pushed himself away from the counter and stretched. "But those strips are fairly pricy and the customer usually prefers cheap stickers that he can buy for next to nothing per thousand. Protectors are used only for special stamps, or for new ones when the gummed sides should remain undamaged."

Saito closed the album, stuck it under his arm, and bowed.

"No tea?" the dealer asked. "My tea is famous in the street. A cup will do you good, especially when you have to face the cold again."

Saito had reached the door. "Thank you," he said, bowing once again. "Some other time perhaps. I appreciate your help."

Saito stopped outside to enjoy the fresh air before walking on, past show windows that held stamps and their appurtenances. A sign dangling from iron hooks reminded him it was lunchtime.

The small restaurant's interior was crowded but he managed to find an empty stool and ordered a dish of fried rice garnished with pickled radish.

He observed the customers while he ate. Most were elderly gentlemen drinking tea and nibbling seaweed cookies while they discussed the contents of each others' stockbooks. Stamps held by tweezers flitted across the tabletops. The cafe seemed to house an eternal exchange. A poster attached to the counter propagated a stamp magazine and informed the public that single copies were available. Saito asked the waitress to bring him the magazine and he glanced through the pages while he slurped his tea. Except for some articles, illustrated with color photographs of stamps, the magazine contained a number of advertisements offering the services of mailorder companies and specialty stores. He saw that the Kyoto-based dealers preferred a certain street, the street he happened to be on now. He sighed and redlined the ads, a total of eight—hopefully he had enough time. He paid, grasped the album under his arm, and left the restaurant.

Fortune smiled at the fifth store. The owner, a small fat fellow with a kindly face, bowed helpfully. "Yes, Inspector, I do remember a repaired lilac, twenty-sen stamp of 1874. I found it in a box with leftovers I picked up cheaply at an auction and I jumped for joy."

Saito grinned. "Before you saw that the stamp was worthless."

The owner whacked himself on the forehead. "Indeed. What a disappointment! The chance you've been praying for and heaven frowns on you after all."

"What did you do with the stamp?"

"I kept it as a curiosity for a while but then I gave it away to a student who had been helping out here for a few weeks. He was a bit of a collector himself and he craved the stamp because it would give some color to an otherwise empty page."

"Do you remember his name?"

The owner's skull had to be thick for the resounding slap he cheerfully gave himself hardly made him blink. "You're a policeman, I clean forgot. That nice young man wouldn't be in trouble, I hope?"

Saito's smile faded away. "He could very well be. Is he a friend of yours?"

"Not a friend," the owner said, "but he was a hard worker and I liked him. His name was Wakana. He told me he was a student of mathematics..."

Ikemiya pointed disdainfully at the stamp Saito had placed on his desk.

"That miserable little rag? Three and a half million yen?"

"Yes, sir—the price of a good-sized house in a nice area or a sum that properly invested will keep a modest man going just on the interest. You must admit that a valuable object like this could consitute a motive for murder."

Ikemiya indicated the chair that he reserved for important visitors. "Sit down, Inspector, and tell me exactly how you concluded your case. I take it that the report and signed confessions will reach me in due course, but we might go through the case verbally now. Fire away, Saito-san."

Saito relaxed in the leather-upholstered seat. "First of all, I should state that I would never have considered the case if Kobori hadn't insisted I should. My visit to Mr. Nogi's house only confirmed Kobori's original suspicion. Setsuko's blatant lie about Nogi-san's drinking habits was the next indication and I began to suspect that the murderers—"

Ikemiya's protesting hand slapped down on the desk blotter. "One moment, Saito. I don't follow how you could, at that early stage of the game, surmise that Setsuko hadn't acted alone."

Saito smiled. "*Parallel Cases under the Peartree*, the Thirteenth Century manual I habitually use when I busy myself with detection. I'll fetch it if you like and read you the relevant passage."

Ikemiya waved the suggestion away. "Save yourself the effort."

"Even in the old days," Saito said solemnly, "magistrates knew that certain kinds of weak, dependent women, and Setsuko is a classic example of the type, do not easily commit serious crimes by themselves. If they do misbehave, a male master has set them off, using them as an accomplice. When I interrogated Setsuko I could see she had little intelligence and that she would have played a lesser part in the drama. She would have met a great many men when she worked as a porno-model and not all elderly gentlemen like Mr. Nogi. I assumed that she had found a lover and the affair had continued after she moved in with Nogi."

"A supposition," Ikemiya said bad-temperedly, "without any factual evidence."

Saito nodded. "Certainly, but a useful hypothesis for the time being. All I had to do was look for facts and try to fit them in with my theory. If they wouldn't fit, the hypothesis would have to be replaced by another."

"Yes, save me the lecture. What happened then?"

"I heard that a young man had been visiting the Nogi residence and that the master of the house had called him both intelligent and eager to learn. I asked myself what Nogi, a retired clerk, could possibly have had to teach him. The old man's only hobby was stamp collecting. It seemed clear that he had showed off his album and this Wakana had shown considerable interest."

Ikemiya's fingers drummed on the blotter. "Right—very possible."

"So the lover and his beloved killed old Mr. Nogi to benefit from the situation. But what did Mr. Nogi own? A house and furniture—objects that are hard or impossible to steal. A stamp album which had not been taken. I took the collection to an expert who told me the only really valuable stamp, an 1874 twenty-sen lilac chrysanthemum, was damaged and therefore worthless while all other stamps were in excellent condition."

"So you had to find the original. And you did for it is here on my desk. How did you find it?"

"I called on the local stamp stores and a dealer told me he had once given a torn 1874 twenty sen stamp to a student of mathematics who had worked in his store. He gave me his name and I telephoned the university and obtained his address. I then collected Sergeant Kobori and we went to Wakana's rooming house."

"Was he there?"

"Yes," said Saito. "He refused to let us in his room at first, saying we should have a warrant, but I threatened to arrest him."

"So you knew the stamp would be in his room."

"Clearly—why refuse to let us in otherwise? The trouble was exactly where in his room? Stamps are easily hidden: Fortunately, Kobori is an experienced policeman and he observed Wakana while I asked him some innocent questions. He noticed that Wakana's eyes kept shifting to a photograph of Setsuko. The photograph probably dated back to the time she worked at the studio because her pose was rather revealing. There were other pictures in the room and Wakana must have seen this photograph a thousand times but its presence seemed to disturb him somehow."

"The stamp had been stuck to the photo's back?"

"We found it in the frame, between the actual photo and a piece of cardboard backing."

Ikemiya grinned contentedly. Did he confess straight off?"

"He refused to say anything for a while but broke down when here in this building I had him look through a cell-door peephole. His spirit broke when he saw Setsuko."

"Did you tell him she had confessed?"

Saito sat up. "I certainly did not—such methods are beneath my sense of dignity."

"But you didn't tell him she had *not* confessed, right?"

"I didn't tell him anything at all. I only wanted him to realize we had arrested his accomplice as well."

"Not to tell the truth is to lie, Saito, but never mind that subtle point for now. We all know that suspects can easily be manipulated when kept in uncertainty. Now tell me how the actual murder was committed."

"Wakana and Setsuko grabbed hold of Mr. Nogi and forced him to drink half a bottle of strong saki."

"So he really had stopped drinking?"

"Yes, and after a year of abstention and with an ulcerous stomach such a dose can be deadly."

"But why didn't they steal the album outright? It was their intention that the house would burn—they couldn't know a neighbor would pick that evening to admire the moonlight."

Saito nodded. "That point bothered me too. But Wakana is a vain young man and he took pleasure in supplying me with an answer. His landlady once asked him to burn some trash in the yard. The trash contained an old telephone book. He learned that a fat book does not disappear in a fire but changes into a lump of brittle ashes that keep the original shape of the volume. Wakana was worried that Mr. Nogi's nephew, the heir, would try to find the album's remnants to claim the value with the insurance company."

Ikemiya sighed and picked up the stamp. "Quite. And how did the suspect intend to change this into money?"

"He was going to wait until the next large stamp auction in Tokyo. Those auctions not only attract dealers but also wealthy collectors. He would have been sure to obtain the full price."

Ikemiya got slowly to his feet. "I believe I have to congratulate you after all, Saito, even if you were incredibly lucky and your hypothesis had little to support it."

Saito stood, bowed, and started for the door. "Wait," the Chief Inspector said, holding out the stamp. "Take this with you before I sneeze and it's lost forever."

Ellery Queen's Mystery Magazine, 1982

Trumpetbird in the Cop Car

The patrol car was sluggish again that night long ago, in the era when police mechanics still repaired rather than replaced, and the Volkswagen shook and rattled every time the clutch was let out. At first the Inspector pulled faces. But after a while he responded by cursing, and when the shaking got worse he wanted me to swear, too. I did, every time. I was a constable then and lower ranks follow when officers guide the way.

The Inspector was a rat-faced gnome, but the two silver stars on his jacket shoulders changed him into a gentleman, never mind his looks— or his behavior, for that matter. My colleagues didn't care to serve under him, for the Inspector liked to look for trouble, but that particular night he seemed friendly enough. His foul language sounded almost tender as I obediently mumbled my repeats from the observer's seat as the car shook along through Amsterdam's empty alleys.

It was late at night with nothing much going on. The radio summoned another car to take care of a bar fight and we headed for the address, too, but it was all over when we finally got there. Broken glass on the floor, and subdued clients staring at the glass while our colleagues lectured the bums on good manners. We saluted both parties and were back on our way.

We found a person of pleasure soliciting close to the Queen's very own Palace. A clear crime. Prostitutes are supposed to ply their trade in the Red Quarter, not where the Queen herself can snoop at them from her very own bathroom. We arrested Suspect, who turned out to be male, dressed in a dress, silk stockings, and high heels—most confusing. How to fill in the form? He/she explained it all—how he/she got that way and whatnot. The Inspector wandered off toward the canteen while I listened and nodded. "Right, dear." I had the form filled in after a fashion and he/she could be on his/her way again, but not before all the story was told. So I listened and sympathized. Why not?

By the time I got to the canteen, the coffee machine had broken down and the Inspector grabbed his hat. I made him wait outside until I was done with my soda, but when I folded myself back into the car I understood I'd better do something helpful.

"Motorcycle!" I shouted and pointed out the speeding machine. "Over there, sir—just passed a red light! Registration V for Victory, R for Roger. The number is unclear. Brand, Honda. Color, green. There he goes, sir, into the Palace Alley!"

"Yes, constable," the Inspector said and made the car turn away. "Not for us. This car's a bit slow."

I knew my duty and grabbed the microphone. Within ten seconds the message came back, directed at all cars. "Catch the green Honda. Victory. Roger."

"Waste of effort," the Inspector snarled. "No one listening but us. The colleagues are out of the their cars, crowding the coffee machines in their respective stations. Quiet night, isn't that right, constable, old chap? The civilians have switched off their tubes and are ready for bed. Anything good on tonight?"

I said I didn't know, I didn't own a TV.

"So what do you do at night? You're not even married, isn't that right?"

I told him about my cat, leaving the bookcase and the record player out. The Inspector is rather down on culture.

He wasn't listening, holding up a small hand. "Hear *that*?"

I heard. A loud two-toned signal, but not the regular wail employed by us cop cars. "A siren, sir."

"Right! A bleeping siren. Where, constable, where?"

I pointed. "The silver Buick, sir, over there. There he goes again."

The siren called nastily in the almost empty square. The Buick faced a green light but was blocked by a compact suffering from starting troubles.

"*Right!*" The Inspector made our car jump. "That bleeper is done for! Sirens are illegal in all nonofficial cars!"

The Buick reversed, circumvented the stalled compact, and moved off at speed. A big truck, popped up from nowhere, got in our way. The Inspector made the VW climb the sidewalk and a kissing couple had to jump out of our way. I didn't foresee a successful pursuit and suggested informing the radio room. "This lemon can't catch a supercar, sir."

My superior knew a variety of four-letter words. I pushed the unused microphone back and steadied myself against the car roof. A lot of trouble, to be totally unrewarded. A misdemeanor, worth twenty guilders maybe—what was it to us if the Buick bully hid a siren in his automated chariot? Did we have to turn ourselves into heroes, run risks, and frighten the innocent populace to catch him? I saw us headed straight for an old man crossing the street. When I opened my eyes again and looked round, the pedestrian had embraced a lamppost. I cursed the car's enthusiasm, for the clutch suddenly worked again and the speedometer was veering far to the right. If there had been a constable at the wheel, I would have pulled out the key.

I reached for the button controlling the car's top lights and siren. The Inspector knocked my hand away. "Leave that—the bastard isn't aware he's being followed yet."

"Sir," I whispered.

The Volkswagen produced a feeble grumble and actually managed to pass the Buick. I extended an arm through the window and moved it up and down in a stately and commanding fashion. The Buick put on her brakes and slowed to a halt. The Inspector jumped out and ran back to face the vast driver who had gotten out, too, his fluffed and hairsprayed mane shining in the lamplight. Under his mangy lion's head I detected a three-piece tailormade suit and the latest fashion turtleneck sweater.

Suspect was known to me. I marched back, too, and noted that I outsized him, which was good. Suspect was upset, just like the Inspector, but my presence seemed to calm both parties somewhat. I folded my hands behind me and arranged my facial expression, aiming for a suitable combination of curiosity and friendliness.

"So what the hell?" Suspect hissed. "So what the hell, hey?"

"Papers," the Inspector yapped.

I checked Suspect's papers. They were quite in order. The Suspect was about to get back into his car when the Inspector growled, "Just a moment. You got a siren in your vehicle. Open up the hood."

"Never," Suspect said. "I ain't got nothing and I don't show nothing. I'm taking my girl friend home and you're hassling me. Let's have your name and rank so I can complain to your chief." He checked the stars on the Inspector's shoulders. "On your way, constable, get back in your wreck."

The Inspector hopped. His short arms waved and his hands had become little fists. "Mouthy, eh? You're under arrest! Get in your sleazy rustbucket and follow us to the station. If you try to get away, every cop car in town will be after you and I'll have you for escape. Constable, make a note of that car's registration."

I handled notebook and ballpoint, put them away again, and saluted.

"So what do you have on me?" The Suspect asked, spittle dribbling down his chin.

"That siren. We'll have a mechanic tear it out and we'll confiscate it."

The Buick followed quietly. It wasn't far. The Inspector grinned and drummed his fingers triumphantly on the wheel.

"Suspect is known to you?" I asked.

"Known now."

"Blond Freddie," I said. "A pimp by trade. He used to keep a few better-looking girls behind windows, but he's come up in the world, runs a smart, cheap nightclub now. The Pink Balloon, in the Mad Nun's Alley."

The Inspector laughed and nodded at the microphone. "Better and better. Let's hear what's in his file so we can weight the charge a bit."

There was nothing down on Suspect right now, but the radio room said Freddie had recently been in jail. Three months for pushing a client around. Severe physical damage. Another three months suspended.

"Nice," the Inspector said. "Very nice indeed. I'll shake him loose in a minute. If he pulls back for a swing, we'll soften his skull."

We had arrived, which saved me an answer.

I unfolded out of the car and banged on the sliding door next to the station. We're next door to the Police Garage, which can be handy at times. The doors veered open a bit and a bearded head stared.

"Open up, colleague, we've got a job for you."

"At this time of night?" the police mechanic complained.

I kicked the door. It finally slid away.

The Volkswagen burbled inside and the Buick flowed after it.

Blond Freddie got out and made an effort to look fierce.

The mechanic released the hood of the Buick and pushed it up.

"Right there," the Inspector shouted, "behind the radiator. Remove that stupid gadget."

The mechanic found the right wrench and released a nut. He wasn't in a hurry and I got a bit bored. I took a look at the Buick and saw the woman inside. She smiled a greeting, but I only saw her mouth—the rest of her face hid behind sunglasses, big ones. I liked her mouth and her thick brown hair, but I mostly noticed her blouse. The tight garment barely contained a majestic cleavage, pearly white in the neon light of the garage lamps. The lady wanted to get out and I opened the Buick's passenger door, putting on my best smile.

The mechanic paused before attacking the next nut and whistled. He seemed to be impressed by the woman's legs, which were long and tightly shaped. I was a constable first class, with one more stripe on each sleeve, so I stared him down and he got back to work. He knocked the little black box containing the siren free with the tapping wrench and handed it to the Inspector.

"Mine," Freddie pleaded. "Cost me money."

"City property now," the Inspector barked. "All ours, until we auction it off. Come along, it's time to fill in your ticket. There's the office! Forward, *march!*"

The woman looked at me. "Sir?"

She'd obviously dealt with the police before. Politeness pays off. We react well to respect.

I straightened up. "Miss?"

"Could you direct me to the restroom?"

The mechanic jumped. "Over there, Miss, behind the motorcycles. Let me show you the way."

She kept looking at me, so I gently pushed the mechanic aside.

She shivered when she passed the motorcycles. Our motor cops are tough. When they catch a punk, they cut off Suspect's hair, dip it in red paint, and attach the bloody hair to a piece of linen. The scalp gets hooked to the radio antennae on their bikes.

"It isn't real blood, " I said.

She pointed at a kid's wrecked cart, crushed a few days ago by a truck in the city. The wreck was splattered with reddish stains. "That isn't real, either," I said. I often lie so that things may look better.

I showed her the restroom door but she didn't go in. "Can I speak to you, sir?" I waited. The others couldn't see us, the corridor has a bend. "Can I trust you?"

I nodded. I'm the public's trusted servant.

She took off her sunglasses. One eye was swollen badly. The discolored bruise petered out in a deep scratch.

"Freddie?" I asked.

An impressive tear ran slowly down her face.

"I see." I kept my voice flat. I'd only had a few years on the force then, but they were bad enough and I hardened a bit—always stay calm, it's less fatiguing and makes it easier for everyone around.

"He's a pimp," she said. "He lives off my sin. That's illegal, right?"

I agreed.

She was thinking. She smiled at me again, without replacing the glasses. "It's a crime," she said softly, "and you can do something if there's a complaint."

She was right, of course, and she had listened to a lawyer—or to one of us. Policemen are clients of the Red Quarter, too.

"Sure," I said. "Will you give us a complaint?"

They usually don't or retract the charge later.

"Yes," she said firmly.

"Will you throw in physical abuse?" That's a nice charge, it makes the judge look up.

"Yes," she said again. "Poor Freddie'll be all yours."

Her good eye looked at me hard. Maybe she sensed my hesitation. I would do all the paperwork and then she'd back out.

"Are you sure now?" I asked.

She turned and unbuttoned her blouse. I saw her back and the long wounds where the skin had broken, swollen up at the edges. "His belt," she said. "Last night. Because I asked for some money. I bring in enough and he keeps it all. He doesn't feed me well."

"Any proof?" I asked. It could be a customer's belt.

"Fred's belt," she said. "The one he's wearing now."

She buttoned her blouse again. She had no need to go to the restroom. When she started to walk past me, I put out a restraining hand.

"Freddie isn't nice. We'll lock him up and he'll get out again. He'll remember the complaint. Some ladies finish up floating in a canal."

"I know. I won't be here. My passport is Belgian. I'll be going home."

"I'll take the case," I said.

I think Freddie knew what had happened between us. When the lady and I walked into the office, he grabbed hold of her. "Couldn't you hold your trap, silly sod?"

He had pulled back his arm, but I caught it before his fist connected. My other hand was flat and hit his head with a whap. The Inspector kicked his shins and the mechanic banged about with his wrench. Even so, Freddie didn't go down straight-away and we had to apply force before he kisssed the floor and we could snap on the irons.

"All done, sir," I panted.

The Inspector sneered back at me with joy.

"And more charges, sir. Pimping and abuse."

The lady repeated herself, without looking at Fred. Fred protested a bit but the lifted wrench shut him up.

"Confiscate the belt," the Inspector said. "Don't handle it too much. Put it in a box so the laboratory can test the blood. Take the victim along. I'll throw Suspect into our worst cell and it'll be home for me after that." He grinned at me. "You're an intellectual—you phrase the report."

Freddie was marched off, prodded by the Inspector's stick. Suspect slouched and looked much worse for wear. I drove the lady to Headquarters, in a car supplied by the mechanic. The lab people took their time with the belt while they stared at my catch. They dallied taking her blood. I took her home afterward. She lived in a dingy room at the rear of the nightclub. She didn't want to stay. I waited for her to pack her bag and took her to a boarding house tucked away in a suburb. She moved close to me in the car and put her hand on my knee.

"Will you be looking me up?"

"Maybe," I said.

"When?"

I said I didn't know yet.

She kissed my cheek and I dented the car's fender on the way back, scratching a lamppost. Policemen should keep themselves apart from the public, but I'd been living alone for over two years, not counting the cat. The cat naps in my arms sometimes but I've been restless, anyway.

I returned the car to the police garage. The mechanic was still on duty. He seemed amused. "You want to hear something?"

"Let's have it," I said.

The Buick's siren was attached to a wire and he unwound it into the street. When he pressed the switch, the siren howled softly. He turned up the volume and the screeching increased, blotting out the quiet of night, then sank back again and cut off with a low gurgle. She mechanic raised a hand. "Listen, colleague."

I heard the siren again, softer and from a distance.

The mechanic pointed at the trees across the road. "You know what's behind there?"

"The zoo," I said.

"There's something horrible out there," the mechanic said, "and I never knew it."

"Keep sounding it," I said, "I'll find out what answers."

Policemen have the right of way, and the zoo's watchman let me through the gate. The mechanic made Freddie's siren howl and I tracked the response. The watchman, a sharp-faced young man, came along.

We found the bird together. The nameplate on the cage lit up when I shone my flashlight. *Psophia Viridis*.

"Trumpetbird," the watchman said. "South American origin, *muy macho*." He told me he studied biology and worked nights at the zoo to help pay for his tuition. I looked at the specimen in the cage, determining the bird to be scraggly and possessed by a furious temper. He faced me bravely, the chicken-sized demon, before attacking the fence and scratching the earth, all hepped up to bury his beak in my throat.

I nudged the watchman "What's up with him?"

"It's the Siren that gets to him," he explained. "Male competition? Would you be trespassing on his turf?"

It was true that the bird calmed down when the mechanic got tired of playing with Freddie's gadget. He seemed ready to go back to sleep.

The watchman invited me into his shed. Daylight broke and I

stayed for coffee, sharing my adventure and inviting the student's comments. He kept grinning at me.

"Amusing?" I asked. "A little weird maybe? You like battered women?"

"Don't you see?" he asked.

"See what?"

"That, as usual, reality is not what we think it is? You're a cop—you think you serve, do a good job, that you care for others, right?"

"I don't?" I asked.

"Bah." The student shrugged. "You and your ratty Inspector. The Police. You lord it over us. The city is yours. You sound off your sirens as proof of your power. Now the other guy, ferocious Fred, contests your power. He sounds his siren and has the audacity to put his paws on a lovely lady. All our ladies are yours."

"Now now," I said.

He was still grinning. "Sex and uniforms. Look at yourself. Six feet four of official bully. Shiny buttons. A gun ready to draw."

I let that go. Civilians sometimes like to poke fun at us. We usually get them later.

"So?" I asked, encouraging him to have his full say.

"Biologists observe nature," the watchman said. "We watch and try to see the truth."

"*We* are the truth," I said. "We uphold it. We represent the state."

"Yes, sir," he said. "You keep proving your strength. You beat the other fellow down, clink him in irons, drag him to a drafty cell, and then you take his woman, your rightful prey."

"Didn't she offer herself?"

He became thoughtful. "The female always manipulates the situation. She wants a strong mate, the fellow who is on top. She has to keep the species going."

I left. He walked me to the gate and suggested I should enjoy myself.

"Well?" the Inspector asked the next day. "Did you have a good time? Didn't I throw you nice spoils? Remember, Constable, the next one will be mine."

Ellery Queen's Mystery Magazine, 1979

The Murders in the Alley of the Mad Nun

"He's still there," Detective-Constable First-Class Gardozo said. "I noticed him in exactly the same spot half an hour ago. There, under the half-dead elm tree. See him?"

Detective-Adjutant Grijpstra looked, "Yes."

"Stares into the water. All the time. Doesn't even move his hands. Would there be anything to see there?"

Grijpstra grunted. "Of course. There's always something. A rubber or two. Empty cans. Seagull on a log." He walked on, stopped when he felt that the constable wasn't with him, turned and ambled back. The adjutant didn't mind wasting a bit more time, they weren't doing anything in particular. Officially they were on patrol, to see that everything was well in the busy red-light quarter of Amsterdam, the city that employed them and three thousand other policemen to maintain order and assist those in need of help.

The two men, now a quiet island in the stream of sex-hungry males floating through narrow alleys and along canal quays, could be taken for father and son, or strangely matched acquaintances representing different layers of Amsterdam society. Grijpstra, in his neat pinstriped suit, would be the ideal citizen, although it might be hard to explain what had taken this portly gentleman to the crossing of the Alley of the Mad Nun and the Straight-Tree Ditch, a notorious trouble spot in the inner city. Cardozo, thirty years younger, fitted the environment better—with his tousled eager head and crumpled corduroy jacket, loose gait and furtive glances at the half-naked women in their display windows all around, the constable might be a student on his way to spend the best part of his monthly allowance. He *was* a student in fact, learning the art of detection, and the adjutant was supposed to teach him.

"What is the fellow looking at?" Cardozo asked plaintively.

"Hmmm?" The adjutant concentrated on lighting a small black cigar. Cardozo coughed when the smoke reached his delicately curved nose. He tugged the adjutant's sleeve. "Really, Adjutant, I don't understand. It's difficult to be that still, especially for any length of time; I know, for I've often tried it. Maybe he's in some kind of coma. Shouldn't we make him move on? Look at those guys over there, with the leather jackets and the rings through their ears. Punks. Trouble makers. They'll sneak up and give him a push, just to see what'll happen. If he falls into the canal he'll hurt himself, or he'll catch some nasty disease. Can I go over and talk to him?"

"No." Grijpstra's restraining hand rested on the constable's shoulder. "But I tell you what you *can* do. Take me over to that nice corner café and buy me a fat sausage and a cup of coffee. It's break-time. Maybe I'll tell you a story then, and give you some information on what goes on here. It'll be an involved story, for it contains four corpses, but if you listen carefully you might learn something. Okay?"

Cardozo considered the proposition. "I pay?"

"Yes."

"A murder story?"

"Three murders, one suicide."

"Recent?"

"Very."

Gardozo pulled a face. "You sure? How come I know nothing about any murders here, recent murders, that is? I read all the reports, every day, I always come early so that I can catch up before getting into the routine."

Grijpstra smiled patiently. "Because there were no murder reports."

"You let it go? Did we slip up? Aren't we the murder squad?"

Grijsptra chuckled. "You and me, and a dozen others. No, no, son, we didn't slip up. But that man over there is the living proof that we don't have to sprinkle salt on every tail. Some cases take care of themselves." The adjutant poked Cardozo's chest with two fingers. "The police maintain order. We don't disturb it. Some stuff should be left alone. We left this alone." He pointed . "Your man survived the story, maybe he shouldn't have, but that isn't our concern. We're guardians, not guardian angels."

Cardozo studied his subject again before he allowed himself to be pushed into the café. "He looks half-dead. Is he?"

"Yes." Grijpstra said. "Hello, miss. A nice sausage, a toasted bun, coffee. Same of my friend. One check please."

"Describe our man," Grijpstra said a few moments later, when he was done mopping up the sausage's gravy with the last piece of his bun.

Cardozo looked out of the window. "Male. White. Six feet tall, but no more than a hundred and fifty pounds. Somewhere in his middle twenties. Seems he's been sleeping in his clothes for a while and hasn't washed much. Hasn't been near a barber for at least a month."

"A bum?"

Gardozo hesitated.

"A drunk? A junkie?"

Cardozo looked again. "Could be a junkie. I would say that he's a student and comes of a good family. He's got some class left. Lots of students live in this quarter, the lofts of the gable houses go cheap, for the whores' customers don't like to climb a lot of narrow straight stairs. Yep, he's a student and he lives in a loft, not far from here." He turned to the adjutant. "Am I right?"

"You're doing fine. What else can you tell me?"

Gardozo shrugged, then thought. "I think the guy is crazy. What did he do? Kill his girl-friend? But you said there were *four* corpses. That's a massacre." He shook his head. "From here on it's all conjecture, you have to fill me in, Adjutant." He imitated the programmed voice of a computer. "Not-enough-data—not-enough-data."

Grijpstra nodded. "Okay, here we go. What you see there is half of a team and the other half is no longer with us. The other half was a little fellow by the name of Ricky, what's left now is called Robert. Ricky is dead because he thought he could fly. He could fly all right, but only down. Seven stories down and *plop*. Isn't it strange that they always go *plop* when they hit the cobblestones? You'd think that you would be able to hear the bones break, a snapping sound, like, but there's just the *plop*, a sort of soft splash."

"Flew down?"

"Just like the nun who named the alley. Know the story?"

"No."

"You should. The city's history is interesting, Constable, the past explains the present. Here's the story. During the seventeenth century the alley was still a field and there was a retreat here, a tall building with a stone courtyard around it. The retreat was filled with nuns, holy women who were trying to outpray each other. This nun was a winner. She counted ten times more beads than her sisters and she mumbled while she counted. So, of course, she became a saint. She had wonderful visions and she developed miraculous powers. Or so she thought."

"Ah."

"Ah is right. But the other nuns, being slow and sinful, irritated the saint, so she killed the lot of them. And then, when she was done, she flew away."

"Up or down?"

"Down. Whoops!—into the courtyard."

"Plop?"

"Right."

"And this Ricky imitated the past?"

"In a way. Ricky is the fourth corpse in my story. The first belonged to a girl who used to live around here, a nice girl from the provinces."

Grijpstra became quiet. Cardozo flapped his hands nervously. "Go on, Adjutant, how come the nice girl is dead? Was she a whore?"

"A hobby-whore. Didn't sit in the window but lived quietly upstairs. Got herself picked up every now and then so that she could choose her clientele. A good girl originally, but when the company for which she typed folded she drifted into the free life."

"On drugs?"

"I found no evidence to that effect. She didn't pick up her mail and milk for a few days, the neighbors alerted the police, and I had the door forced. Girl by the name of Anne. She was in her bed."

"Dead?"

"Yeh, not too long. Two days, maybe. The doctor came and we had tests done and the white-coats went crazy. A rare drug, North African snake poison, bizarre. There was a bit left in a small funny-looking bottle, and the rest was in her stomach and blood. The poison causes death by slow paralysis, apparently painless. Everybody was excited."

"You too?"

Grijpsta sighed. "At my age? But I did some work, I can still work. The girl had no North African friends, she didn't have any friends at all, except two students, Robert and Ricky, who lived in the top apartment of the building across the street. They got to know each other by waving, then met in the street, started visiting, going out together, shared weekend breakfasts; friends, you know, friends."

"Ricky and Robert weren't homosexuals?"

"Not all the way, there was room for the other side."

"Were they Anne's lovers?"

"Ricky more than Robert."

"How do you know all that?"

Grijpstra waved the question away. "Enquiries, with the neighbors, the shop-owners around here, this café where we are now. I also checked with the university where Robert and Ricky studied. They were both in their fourth year reading psychology, doing well. Would have had their masters' degrees in another two years. Brilliant students."

"Right."

Grijpstra raised his eyebrows. "Do you know which way I'm going?"

"Not yet, but it sounds good. Go on, Adjutant, please."

"Can't, my throat is dry."

"Milk? We're still on duty."

"Anything."

The milk came. Grijpstra scraped his throat. "Brilliant students. They were travelers, too, spent all their holidays abroad. I got to know them and when I visited their apartment I asked them to show their passports."

Cardozo clapped his hands. "North African rubber stamps."

"Indeed. Algeria. I invited them to come over to the station, and had them in the cell-block for a while. They told me that Anne wanted to commit suicide and that they'd obliged by providing a suitable poison. But the tale didn't quite fit you see. That girl was in fine shape, her room was neat and cozy, there were books, flowers, a TV set, a balcony with all sorts of stuff growing in pots. Not the sort of environment a depressed soul usually projects. Yet she killed herself. Why? Eh?"

"Don't know, Adjutant."

"Neither did 1. She wasn't pregnant, either. But she left a note, saying that she'd done it herself, without any further explanation."

"So?"

"So nothing. I released the suspects. They went home, quite a place by the way, done up in your latest arty style. Thousands of books, good paintings, excellent sound equipment, oriental rugs, the lot."

"One bedroom?"

"One bedroom with one double bed."

"So you figured they hated women and knocked the girl off?"

Grijpstra cleaned his mouth with a napkin. "The thought crossed my mind. They were psychologists, so they could have manipulated the poor thing. Good theory, impossible to prove. I thought I would let it go for a little while, keep in touch and wait for mistakes. There are always mistakes."

"Lets hear the mistakes."

"You know," Grijpsira said *"Histoire se répète*. For ever and ever. That mad nun was an arrogant bitch, but she crashed all the same. The clever are always too arrogant, they learn a little and they think they know it all. I've made the same mistake myself."

Cardozo grinned slyly. "You mean you can levitate too?"

Grijpsira grunted.

"Sorry, Adjutant. A little joke."

"There are moments," Grijpstra said gently, "that I approve of you, there are other moments, however. . ."

"I said I was sorry."

"Now, listen. What did I have? North African venom and two intellectual lads who like to vacation in Algeria, hang around the kasbah, buy poison. . .What else? A nice dead girl in a nice well-made bed, befriended by my two perverts. What else? A note. I'd have to prove that that note was written under duress, in some subtle form. They stood over her with a whip or something. After Ricky died, Robert broke down and told me what happened. Manipulation, as I thought all the time. The girl, in spite of her neat apartment, flowerpots and so forth, was depressed. Ricky worked on that. He gave her the wrong books, took her to the wrong movies, talked about the wrong subjects. He gradually proved to her that this planet is a hell-hole of pain and disease, of concentration camps, jails and lunatic asylums, that every hour hurts and the last one kills, that we are squirrels trapped in a cage, moving on a revolving wheel that we put into motion ourselves, you're familiar with the theory?"

"I'm Jewish," Cardozo said.

"What does that mean?"

"Jews suffer a lot."

Grijpstra's fist shot out and hit Cardozo's shoulder.

"Ouch! Why are you hitting me?"

"So that you can suffer more. Don't feed me that crap. Suffering isn't exclusive to the chosen people, you know. I suffer too."

"Right, Adjutant. Don't hit me again."

"If you give me no reason I won't. Bah. I'm all for the Jews, but don't tell me all the others have a good time. Shit. Have you had the pleasure of meeting my wife?"

"Is she Jewish?"

"No. If only she would be. She might be intelligent then. She is not . . . She is also obese. She makes *me* suffer."

"Okay, Adjutant. I won't say it again."

"Good." Grijpstra waited until his breath slowed down.

"This Ricky, and frozen Robert over there, but mainly Ricky because he was banging the girl more than Robert, worked on her until she cracked and then suggested suicide, the ideal way out. No man has to take what life thinks it wants to give. And just to prove that he was serious he would go with her."

"They took poison together?"

"*He* drank water. Then he got out of the bed, arranged everything in her apartment so that his presence wouldn't be noted and got the hell out."

"The note?"

"They wrote individual notes. That was Ricky's idea, so that the police wouldn't think anybody was involved. But he took his own note with him."

"And then he flew out of the window; but you said there were *four* corpses; who did the second and third belong to, more girls?"

"No. Ricky had proved his art and Robert had to go one better. At university they were rivals. One successful psychological experiment warrants another."

"What did they call the experiment?"

"The ultimate breakthrough of the superego, do you know the terms?"

Cardozo's forehead wrinkled. "Not quite."

"Superego stands for tradition, the collection of taboos society thinks up to protect itself and make sure it will last forever. *Thou shalt not* and all that. Contemporary social evolution has done away with most taboos, but we still have some left. Most things go now; you can sleep with your mother and curse the queen in public, it's okay to steal from the state; but we haven't quite come to the point that we agree we may kill each other. *Thou shalt not kill*; the last frontier, Constable. Break that and you're in true no-man's-land, free as the great bald eagle. Robert and Ricky meant to liberate themselves to the point where they could soar out of the galaxy. Follow?"

"I think so."

"Try and stay with me. Now it was Robert's turn to crack the castle of superego. He chose his own way, but he had to do better than Ricky, of course, he was going to break the record. He planned to kill twice. Remember those guys you pointed out to me just now? There they go."

"The punks?"

"Right. They're members of a gang here, and they all look the same. Tight black pants, black leather jackets, sunglasses. They shave their heads except for that ridiculous tuft on top, wear chains and so forth. They're tough. They mug and burn and steal and destroy, in a petty way, for they don't have much brain; even so they do their best."

"Bad boys."

"Not too bad. To be evil is an art in itself, but they're trying. Robert studied the gang and its habits and built a trap. He picked one of them up and took him to the apartment when Ricky wasn't there, made love to the follow and paid him off. The punk saw that the apartment was loaded and was bound to tell his friends. The punks like a bit of burgling every now and then, and damage what they can't take with them."

"Hm, hm," Cardozo said now, "I remember *that* report; the spray-can?"

"Exactly. Robert was all set up for what would happen. He'd met a soldier of fortune in Algeria who turned out to be an explosives expert. For money he made a paint spray-can into a bomb. If anyone were to touch its button the bomb would go off; there was a safety switch on it somewhere so that it could be transported. Robert bought two spray-cans filled with black paint, and the mercenary worked on one of them. Robert put the cans on the apartment dining-table, left the door off the latch and went out."

"The punks sneaked in, found the spray-cans, had fun with one of them and..."

"Blew themselves up with the other. But not completely. There was enough TNT in that can to tear most of the roof off. I couldn't believe the mess when I saw it. One bookcase covered with black paint, the other with blood. Arms and legs everywhere. One punk's hand got stuck to the ceiling; it dropped down while I stood in what was left of the room right in front of my feet."

"Yakh!"

"Yeh. Wham! Smithereens! But Robert overdid it. Ricky came home late that evening. Ricky may have been a real smart little fellah, but he had weak nerves. The girl died in a quiet way, just slipped into sleep that deepened into death, but what Robert had done was too spectacular. Ricky couldn't stand the scene, went crazy instantly, and jumped through a hole that the bomb had blown into the front wall."

"You were there?"

"No. I had gone home. I arrived just after the explosions and met Robert. He claimed he'd been out for a walk, and suggested that the punks had meant to blow up the apartment with a home-made time-bomb, but that the thing went off too early. There was nothing I could prove. We found shreds of the spray-can, but it didn't occur to me that the can was the bomb. The experts were busy when I left. I had dinner, came back, and thought that this was the next act in the same play, but I didn't get much further than thinking. It was only when Robert had a mental breakdown of his own and sought me out when I happened to stroll through the alley, a couple of days later, that I understood the details.'

"You thought Robert had killed the punks? Before he told you, I mean?"

"Yes. But there was no proof. The proof had exploded as well. That's why I didn't arrest him after the confession."

Cardozo nodded. "I see. A confession on its own is not sufficient proof for conviction. If you had arrested Robert he would have had a chance to reflect in jail, denied the original statement, and accused you of forcing him into saying he'd done it. And his lawyer would have needled you."

"Yes. And there the policeman is in court, stuttering away, and the judge throws the whole thing out. Not guilty because of lack of proof. I've been through that before, not again, not if I can help it."

"So?"

"When in doubt do nothing. I did nothing. I'm still doing nothing."

A long shiver went through Cardozo's small body. Grijpstra stared out of the window. "And there stands our survivor. When I didn't arrest him he managed to survive his attack of guilt, or whatever you would like to call it. His experiment failed. He never broke the superego. But there was much to do. The insurance paid up and he had the apartment rebuilt. Living alone seemed okay, a pleasant change, even, for Ricky had been a trying companion. He studied, and passed more examinations. Then he began to dream."

"How do you know?"

"Because he told me. We run into each other sometimes, or ran; now he doesn't recognize me any more. He would tell me what was going on in his mind. At first there were just the dreams, then there were hallucinations as well. He would meet the punks, Ricky, Anne. He went a little crazy for a while. Talked to himself, gestured. That went away too. Now..."

"Now he stares at the water. Wow! What a way to go. What comes next, Adjutant?"

Grijpstra didn't hear the question. He was watching the two punks. "Hey..."

Cardozo was out of the door first, running lightly. He'd noticed the punks' faces, made up to current fashion, with mascara accentuating their cheekbones and contrasting with the belladonna-glitter of their deepset eyes, half a second after Grijpstra understood what would happen next. Not even Cardozo, a trained runner, was in time to prevent the splash. The punks, their feet shuffling soundlessly, reached Robert and jumped simultaneously. One punk pushed, the other kicked. The body fell. Then the punks were running.

Cardozo made a supreme effort, he no longer seemed to touch the cobblestones. He flew past the first punk and passed him while his hand shot out, clipping the boy neatly under the left ear. He didn't bother to stop to watch his catch fall, knowing that Grijpstra was behind him somewhere to clean up. The second punk made a mistake; he looked over his shoulder to estimate the distance between himself and the pursuing demon, and tripped. Cardozo went into the series of grips necessary to bring a suspect's arms behind his back and attach handcuffs. Then he yanked the suspect to his feet and dragged him back to the spot where Grijpstra was blowing his whistle.

Uniformed policemen arrived, stripped, and dived into the canal. They brought up Robert's body. Two-way radios scratched the heavy air on the quayside; an ambulance backed up, its siren still whining.

"Dead?" Grijpstra asked the car's uniformed attendants.

They knelt and investigated the sodden form.

"Afraid so. There's a wound on the skull, a rather shallow gash I would say. Probably hit some metal junk when he fell in. Wound wouldn't have killed him. Why didn't he swim? Man his age should be able to swim."

"Maybe he didn't want to swim."

"What?"

"He fell in, hurt himself. He fell face downward. If he had turned over he might have been okay. So maybe he didn't want to be okay."

"Whatever," the ambulance driver said. "Your police-talk is always too deep for me. He does look kind of peaceful now."

Grijpstra and Cardozo squatted and studied the dead face. "Very," Grijpstra said, "and so he should." Then he turned to Cardozo. "What you see here, Constable," the Adjutant said kindly, "is a perfect example of a happy end."

Swedish Ministry of Culture prize-winner, 1979

Judge Dee Plays His Lute

personages:

FEMALE VOICE
JANWILLEM VAN DE WETERING (monologues)
JUANITA VAN DE WETERING
PROTESTANT PARSON
ROBERT VAN GULIK
NUDE WOMEN (shuffle their feet)
DAITOKU-JI ZEN MASTER
JAPANESE ZEN MONKS (chant)
GERMAN MAIDS (sing)
LITTLE BOY (sings)
GERMAN SOLDIERS (shout)
KEMPETAI ZEN MASTER
CAPTAIN UYEDA
KEMPETAI SOLDIER
TAMAKI, JAPANESE PUBLISHER
JUDGE DEE
MASTER GOURD
SACRILEGIOUS ZEN-SACRISTAN LU
MR WANG
MISS FU
OLD MAN DZJENG
BUBU (a gibbon)

(A golden wave of sound as a temple bell is struck with a thin copper rod.)

FEMALE VOICE: *Seki no yugiri*
  evening fog on the mountain pass
  Does the temple bell ring?
  Or is this the sound of its clapper?
  The sound has to come from somewhere
  between bell and clapper.

VAN DE WETERING (VDW): Is it the teacher teaching?
  Is it the student learning?
  The insight has to come from somewhere
  between teacher and student.

(The bell sounds again.)

VDW: Teacher - the bell. Student - the clapper. An Eastern image. The student is I, or you. Any one of us is the singular student. But Eastern symbolism distinguishes two kinds of teachers: inside and outside. The inside teacher, the voice within, is eternally present, forever free of illusion. It urges us to become what we always were, are now, will be—our changeless, divine nature.

(The golden bell majestically sounds again. Then, harshly, unexpectedly hardwood boards hit each other. CLASH!)

VDW (change of voice): The inside teacher is a very frightening force. Beware the inner voice for it never gives up. It is the ultimate eternal energy, it uses any temporary energy that happens to be around. The inside guru has no preferences, no morals, it will make use of anything to wake us up, keep us moving. The divine energy uses music. . .

(Voice blends with Miles Davis playing MY LITTLE VALENTINE.)

VDW: Glamorous violence.

(A Harley Davidson is starting up, then another, and another, the motorcycles drive off.)

VDW: The sea.

(Sounds of large waves crashing on a beach.)

VDW: Sexual attraction.

(Female seductive laughter mixing in with the waves.)

VDW: Alcohol, hashish.

(The jazz trumpet enters again, a glass fills with liquid, a water pipe bubbles.)

VDW: Poetry.

(Lovely female voice: a rose is a rose is a rose is a rose. . .)

VDW: War.

(The apparently innocent sound of a helicopter.)

VDW: Inside divinity within uses outside teachers, temporary ever-changing shapes, who accompany us for awhile, guide us here and there, share their own hard-earned insights freely. We all have such teachers. One of mine is called Robert van Gulik. Physically our paths never crossed but I did touch his being twice. Once when he was alive in Japan, once when he was dead in Holland.

(The slow opening of Schubert's DEATH AND THE MAIDEN, as the theme is repeated it becomes background music. We hear the hollow-sounding voice of a parson leading a funeral service.)

PARSON: Brothers and Sisters, we have gathered here today to say farewell to a very special, an exceptional man, a man who distinguished himself as our former ambassador in Japan, as a world-famous sinologue, as a renowned collector of Chinese art, as the internationally known author of the Judge Dee novels, that scholarly yet realistic saga featuring an honest official of genius, set in the T'ang dynasty fighting demonic forces . . .(the voice is ebbing away).

(Once again the first slow movement of DEATH AND THE MAIDEN.)

VDW: I got to know my guide through his many books, novels and learned essays. Van Gulik and I happened to be in the same countries at the same times; I might have run into him but it didn't happen. Maybe better that way. I was afraid that our personalities would irritate each other, it seemed that a bodyless, ephemeral contact might improve my opportunity to learn.

(again the first slow movement of DEATH AND THE MAIDEN.)

VDW: Van Gulik's terminal cancer was induced by nicotine. He was hospitalized in Holland. My wife told me—lunch time.

(Rustling sounds of a newspaper being handled.)

JUANITA: My God, listen to this: "Robert Hans van Gulik, "after a short illness". . ."order of the Japanese imperial chrysanthemum, the Willemsorde". . . will you just look at this list of medals and titles, the funeral service is today, you better go, what time is it? Half past ten? You'll easily make it if you leave now. . .

(more rustling of the newspaper)

Your idol. You must have memorized every letter he ever wrote. He was only 57, isn't that amazing?

VDW (monologue): One's spouse, another divinity-sent guide. The Inner Voice chooses the student's wife to keep his quest moving.

JUANITA: And the other way round, you Dummkopf.

VDW (monologue, chuckling): Who wants to go to a funeral?

JUANITA: Go. GO!

(A car door slams, an engine starts up, ticking of the direction indicator, sounds of the car joining traffic. Schubert's DEATH AND THE MAIDEN, second movement, the sad beginning only, behind VDW's voice.)

VDW: It was autumn 1967—a hot afternoon, I recognized the theme, Schubert's "Death and the Maiden", very appropriate. Van Gulik liked girls. The music must have made me sleepy. Did I close my eyes for a moment? Around the coffin, in time with the composition, moved the exquisite

(Sounds of the Ch'in lute, a seven-stringed Chinese instrument.)

Chinese and Persian women Van Gulik re-created in his Judge Dee books, and that he drew, in the illustrations. The ladies were nude of course. This was great. I am at the funeral of an important diplomat, between all sorts of be-medalled and be-ribboned dignitaries, generals in uniform, Orientals in morning-coats and striped pants, Africans in flowing gowns, elderly ladies all in black, wearing amazing hats, and on the stage around a coffin young nude women dance; shouldn't we be mourning?

(A jazz trumpet blows a few blues notes through the Schubert composition, we also hear nude feet lightly dancing on boards, and hear female whispering. Van Gulik's voice, hoarse, interrupted here and there by dry coughing, he seems amused.)

VAN GULIK: When I shall die?
  Who will remember me in sorrow?
  Only the black mountain crows
  will visit my grave.
  But the crows that fly from the mountain top
  will not feel any sorrow either:
  Except for the funeral cookies that they can't reach
  placed on an altar that celebrates my death.

VDW: The humor of Buddhism. It takes everything away, except for a few cookies that we can't get at and will rot away too. Nothing remains, we are about to realize the famous, or infamous, Buddhist void. Losing everything leads to gaining everthing. There is my teacher, stepping out. Should I ask him whereto? Now that his flame has been snuffed out? No need, that's one of the nice things about hallucination. Instant telepathy.

VAN GULIK : We all return where we came from:
  Where the flame of the snuffed candle died.

VDW: There he is, leaning casually against his own coffin: a tall balding heavy-set man in a tailor-made three-piece suit, puffing on a fat cigar, dropping ashes on his watch chain festooned waistcoat, looking at the audience through comical little round gold-rimmed glasses. As he observes the fading earthly scene he pensively touches his goatee.

(The golden bell sounds again.)

That was the second, the last, time I saw Dr. van Gulik, at the funeral cremation—in Holland we have no room for graves—where I also saw the beings, humans, animals, his books had introduced me to. . .heroes and heroines who, one by one, join him around the coffin. A most wonderful company. But before highlighting these Buddhist masters and Zen tramps, the courtesans and artists, the delicate graceful gibbon monkeys, the contemporary antagonists Meneer Hendriks and the Japanese Military Police Captain Uyeda, all exotic heroes and anti-heroes Van Gulik created to become part of his readers, before I do that let me take you back to our first meeting, the moment when our minds first touched. That was when Dr. van Gulik explained the symbolism of oriental wisdom, that I needed so urgently in my quest for truth, and that this meeting between teacher and student brought about. . .

FEMALE VOICE: Does the temple bell ring?
  Or is this the sound of its clapper
  the sound has to come from somewhere
  between bell and clapper.

(Again the golden sound of the bell, to be rudely interrupted by the sudden clash of hardwood clappers.)

VDW: I was studying at the Japanese Zen monastery Daitoku-ji,—"*Dai*" means "Big", "*Toku*" means compassion, "*Ji*" means temple—(solemnly) The Temple of the Great Compassion. (ironically) Yes, sure. . .Daitoku-ji, a magnificent cluster of T'ang style buildings in Kyoto, spending long, interminable, painful hours in a Zendo, a meditation hall.

(WHACK! A wooden stick hits a human body.)

VDW: The whack of the keisaku, the Zen stick, the only sound permissible in that gloomy place of silent terror. The patrolling monk hits me every time I doze off, or groan with pain. In the Zendo I prepare my mind, to be worthy of being given a koan, a riddle of existence my Zen master expects me to solve in meditation. I am told the koan is a key that opens the lock of ignorance, or a ram that splinters the gate created by my egotistical human misunderstanding.

(WHACK!)

Liberating answers are supposed to pop up from my pain-filled silence,

(A champagne bottle pops.)

bubble up.

(Short phrase on a bamboo xylophone.)

I am told by tough, "cool", American Zen students who visit the temple, that truth appears from the depth of my being as I cut down my thoughts with the sword of the Bhodisatva Manjusri.

(WHACK!)

But the only thing that popped up was a big fly up my asshole in the monastery's smelly latrine. There wasn't much happening when I sat in the Zendo, glowing and crackling legs folded—the pain made them burn slowly—six, sometimes eight hours a day, twenty hours a day for one horrifying week in December. All I ever experienced was a maddening dance of unrelated thoughts in my feverish brain, and if by chance I became too weak to feel pain there would be endless gray boredom, where my feet stuck in mud. . .

(Sounds of boots being pulled out of oozing mud.)

I needed to ask some simple questions about the methods of Zen, but when I tried to gather practical information, the monks answered by chanting sutras, the Buddha's sermons, in a long forgotten formal language,

(Monks' chanting, rhythm is provided by wooden "fish head drums" and gongs. MA-KA-HA-NYA-HA-RA-MI-TA.)

and the monastery's teacher, who received me early in the morning, spoke only Japanese. I heard the same words, morning after morning.

DAITOKU-JI ZEN MASTER (kindly - a pleasant old man's voice): *Jan-san wakaranai. Mada mada. Mo-o chot-to mat-te kudasai. Zazen shiro!*

VDW: Gradually I learned some of the words. The Zen master was saying I didn't understand. Not yet not yet. To wait patiently. To sit quietly in meditation. And then. . .

(A small handbell is rung rapidly by the master.)

To get out of his sight. Orders are orders. No more questions. I was ordered back to the Zendo, where the keisasku, the meditation stick, was waiting

(WHACK!)

or the flies in my room.

(buzzzzzz...The buzzing is ended by a small gong being touched lightly, then there is festive drumming and cheerful Japanese voices, children's voices, young women's laughter.)

VDW: There will be days off. The monks entertain their guests. As I am no monk I don't have to do any entertaining either. I call myself a student of philosophy, no partying for the studious. I have come to Daitoku-ji to find out life's meaning. Wandering about the temple buildings I find a huge library room.

(Creaking of heavy hinges, the acoustics of vast space surrounds my lonely footsteps.)

There are thousands of books, piled everywhere, collecting dust.

(Swishing of books being moved, of hollow foot steps, of coughing as dust swirls.)

Leather bound books, in Chinese, Japanese, Sanskrit, all unreadable. No—wait.

(The ch'in music starts up again.)

Here is a book in English. THE GIVEN DAY. By Robert van Gulik, the first time I see that name. On the cover

(The Ch'in melody changes into a schlager, a sad waltz, played on Amsterdam street organ, a barrel organ.)

is a man in a raincoat and a felt hat. His clothes are soaked through. He is a tall man, stooped, who looks Dutch. The Dutchman is bowing respectfully to a smaller man in a Japanese army uniform, an officer who carries a long sword.

(Sounds of a bamboo flute join the street organ's sad schlager.)

The author's photograph is on the back of the book's dust cover. While the monastery's party is going on outside I read in the library. Fatigue facilitates hallucination. So does a diet of a little boiled barley and a little seaweed. In the Daitoku-ji library Van Gulik himself appears and I see that he is a big burly man, well-dressed. My fellow Dutchman, lighting a long cigar, looks down at me, smiling.

(Sound of a match being struck, a man sucking smoke.)

VAN GULIK(coughs): I wrote the book for you. To explain to you what a koan is. You don't know that yet.

VDW: I think I do, of course. A koan is an illogically construed riddle. What is the sound of one hand? Does a puppy dog have the Budha nature? That kind of a question is a riddle that points beyond dualism. Far beyond yes or no. A riddle that has to be answered outside the evaluating ego. In order to answer a koan one steps away from all coordinates. My Zen master wanted to hear me say my answer.

VAN GULIK: He wants to see your answer. You have to show him.

VDW: Yes yes. And how was I to show my new-found detachment to the authorities of Zen?

VAN GULIK: By forgetting.

VDW: And what was I to forget?

VAN GULIK (puffs smoke, coughs): All your clever answers. Like my Meneer Hendriks does after he inherits Captain Uyeda's koan. Captain Uyeda will be hung by the neck until he is dead so that Meneer Hendriks can take over and clear his mind. Clear your mind, my friend.

VDW: Forget to remember.

FEMALE VOICE: To remember
   Is to forget again.
   Don't remember

So you won't have to forget.

VDW: But I remembered. One early morning Daitoku-ji's teacher, the little old Zen master who suffered from Parkinson's disease, and who would soon die, looks at me, smiling...
—Zen masters smile a lot—

DAITOKU-JI ZEN MASTER: Jan-san, why you come all the way from Holland where you are safe behind strong dikes? Why you want practise unpleasant Zen training. You not happy?

VDW: Happiness...Who the hell is happy on this Earth?...Isn't Dostoyewski right? Aren't only children and idiots happy? Before they learn to remember. I was very happy as a child. My mother was away often and I was raised by German maids who sang...

GERMAN MAIDS (merrily): Hoppa hoppa Reiter
   Hop Hop Horseman

LITTLE BOY (merrily): When you fall you cry-ah

GERMAN MAIDS: Fall in the lake

LITTLE BOY: Food for ravens you make

VDW: And cry-ah I did, when the three-engined German Airforce Junkers came fly-ahng in, low over Rotterdam, May 5th, 1940.

(Sound of low-flying aircraft.)

LITTLE BOY: *Fressen ihn die Ra-ben*
   Rotterdam burns.

(Sound of bombs, whistling down, a child cries out in fear.)

GERMAN MAIDS: *Fallt er in den Gra-ben.*

VDW: There is something wrong with the meaning of life, when lovely women sing with you in the kitchen and the next day their brothers drop killing fire from the sky, and kick your little Jewish school friends, seven and eight year olds, into cattle cars at Rotterdam's Railway Station in a train bound for Treblinka death camp.

SOLDIERS (shouting): Schnell schnell! Little shit dogs!

(Sound of a railway engine puffing, children crying.)

GERMAN MAIDS (merrily): Hoppa hoppa Reiter
  Hop hop horseman.

(The railway engine is still audible in the distance.)

VDW: Makes you give up on the idea of a loving god. Like my Zen master must have done when he was a soldier in Manchuria. He told me about that. Being a sickly former monk he wasn't sent to the front.

DAITOKU-JI ZEN MASTER: I always on guard duty (laughs), like this

(Sound of a rifle butt hitting the ground.)

with my rifle (master takes deep breath, exhales, groans) powerful meditation!

VDW: What was he guarding in Manchuria? A prison camp? A poison gas facility? A biochemical warfare laboratory? What was he meditating on? The Buddha's compassion?

DAITOKU-JI ZEN MASTER: Buddha not your uncle, Buddha not a nice man. Buddha lives in Emptiness. No morals in emptiness. No no-morals in emptiness. Buddha free. (laughs). You Buddha. Jan-san Freeman Buddha. What you come see me for?

VDW: Maybe I wanted him to push me into that vast emptiness.

GERMAN MAIDS: Hoppa hoppa Rei-ter. . .
When he falls he cry-ahs. . .

DAITOKU-JI ZEN MASTER: Why cry? (Cheerfully) Yes. Letting go. Good. Fall. Good. Never fall down far enough. (Whispers). If only you could be just lit-tle more negative.

VDW: That was funny. My father always wanted me to be just a little more positive. What I really wanted to be was neither. De-tached.

DAITOKU-JI ZEN MASTER (compassionately): De-tached. Yes, but de-tached still not free enough. De-tached is still something. (Whispers). Push yourself over the edge, Jan-san. (Speaks normally). While you sit still in Zendo, Jan-san.

(Master rings his little hand bell as a sign the meeting is over. Monks continue chanting the Heart Sutra in the distance: SHIN-NGYO-KAN-JI-ZAI-BO-SA-GYO-JIN. . . Again the change-over to Schubert's violins . . . that dies away while Van Gulik clears his nicotine-damaged throat, coughs softly.)

VAN GULIK: Your Zen master is about to give you a koan. But for you things are made easy. In my war novel, Second World War, the Japanese in Java, Meneer Hendriks has a koan too, which he inherits from his torturer, the enemy, Captain Uyeda of the Kempetai, who got it from his Zen master.

KEMPETAI ZEN MASTER (loudly, belly voice, like a samurai chief in a Kurosawa movie):   You, Uyeda-student-san, you do something for me.

UYEDA (obediently):   *Hai!* (meaning "yes").

KEMPETAI ZEN MASTER (Kurosawa voice):   Make the eternal snow on Mount Fuji melt.

(Silence.)

UYEDA: But the snow on Mount Fuji is eternal, *sensei* (teacher).

KEMPETAI ZEN MASTER (Kurosawa voice): Make eternal snow melt. *(The master rings his hand bell.)*

VAN GULIK: Because the Kempetai, the secret sadistic Japanese war police, were trained well, they learned how to interrogate prisoners, how to torture, but also, hopefully, how to be free of illusion, see clearly. The Kempetai student officers were ordered "to do Zen" the tough way.

KEMPETAI ZEN MASTER (big voice): *Zen suru nasai!*

VAN GULIK: Do Zen!

(Sound of the Zen stick hitting a Kempetai student's back. WHACK! groan WHACK! groan WHACK! (this is a real beating) WHACK!)

KEMPETAI ZEN MASTER: Be nothing, for the sake of the rising sun of Nippon, become nothing, be Nothing!

VAN GULIK: The path of glory...but Captain Uyeda's way turned out to be the worm's way.

FEMALE VOICE: Only two ways lead to the Eernal gate:
   Either dig your head in the mud like a worm,
   or floathigh above the this and that
   like a swan, in an azure sky.

(The funeral music starts up again, this time it is Mozart's Requiem, first part of the Introitus, before the singers come in we hear Van Gulik's voice rising through the row of double basses)

VAN GULIK: Better be a swan.

VDW: The nude girls are no longer dancing around my teacher's coffin. I see Meneer Hendriks and the Japanese captain, Meneer

Hendriks is a tall man in a worn wet raincoat, he looks tired, in pain—Captain Uyeda looks smart in his uniform, martial with his brushed up mustache, and the long samurai sword at his side.

VAN GULIK: Meneer Hendriks is the swan, Captain Uyeda is the worm (laughs). Does that surprise you? The last will be the first? Smacks of Christianity does it not?

VDW: Yes yes, I know that. Wisdom is in all the religions. I was reading about Meneer Hendriks' martyrdom in the moanastery's library. Meneer Hendriks is a reserve-officer in the Dutch East Indies Army. The invading Japanese rape and kill Mrs. Hendriks and her daughter. Meneer Hendriks is taken a prisoner. The Kempetai, the Japanese military police, are sure Meneer Hendriks knows important mlitary secrets. . .

UYEDA (coldly):   You think you are the eternal snow on Mount Fuji? You think I can't make you melt? You want to be whipped again, Hendriks-san?

(Swishing of the whip, a scream.)

UYEDA: Well?

HENDRIKS (weakly):   You can whip me to death. I have nothing to lose anymore.

UYEDA (pleasantly): That's a good position to be in. (thoughtfully) Nothing to lose, eh?

HENDRIKS (weakly):   Well, my life, but I don't care about my life.

UYEDA (pleasantly): You know, philosophically speaking, I think that's where the real secret is. Not caring. Maybe my Zen master wanted me to get there?

HEDRIKS: Goddammit, I have no secrets. Never did. How many times must I tell you?

(Whipping, screams.)

KEMPETAI SOLDIER: Be polite to captain-san, you dog.

UYEDA: No, that's all right, soldier-san. Maybe we should stop hurting the prisoner now. Put that whip down.

KEMPETAI SOLDIER: *Hai!*

HENDRIKS: You know you have lost the war, don't you, captain-san. It's just a matter of time now.

UYEDA (coldly):   You mean they will hang me?

HENDRIKS: According to western morals you committed many war crimes.

UYEDA (coldly):   You mean they will hang me?

HENDRIKS: Yes.

KEMPETAI SOLDIER (nervous):   Shut up! Prisoner dog!

UYEDA (pleasantly): I did have a dog, Hendriks-san. He was a nice dog. We loved each other. Love is pain. Love keeps me shackled to life and suffering. I thought that my love for Dog-chan would keep me from making the eternal snow on Mount Fuji melt. (thoughtfully). . . yessss, yessss . . . So I scratched Dog-chan between his ears with my bayonet. Dog-chan liked that. And then I cut his throat.

(Silence.)

HENDRIKS (softly): That's Zen?

UYEDA: I thought so.

HENDRIKS: You better cut my throat too. When the British come and if I am freed I have nothing to go back to. You killed my family, wrecked my mind and body. What do I want with my freedom?

UYEDA: Killing Dog-chan didn't melt Mount Fuji's eternal snow. Cutting your throat won't do it either, Hendriks-san. I didn't solve my koan. I failed.

(A cymbal is touched softly.)

VAN GULIK (coughs): The British condemned Captain Uyeda. (coughs) Meneer Hendriks came to say goodbye to his tormentor, to wish him well in the next life. He said he bore no grudge. Uyeda thanked Hendriks, then passed on his koan, just before the noose slipped around the Kempetai captain's neck.

VDW: I see Uyeda and Hendriks standing next to each other, facing the coffin. They seem happy together. They should be. Van Gulik's book has a happy end.

VAN GULIK: Sharing the koan torturer and tortured became each other, and then Hendriks solves the koan and frees them both. And thereby everybody. You too. (Coughs) And me.

(Music on the Ch'n lute.)

FEMALE VOICE: Being born means to have to suffer.
   Living and Suffering are identical ideas.
   Dying, and never being born again
   Is the only way out.
   The final way out, away from unpleasantness,
   from pain.

(Schubert: DEATH AND THE MAIDEN, a passage where double basses dominate, but then the music lightens up, oriental notes lead us to the dance.)

VDW: There was a glint in Van Gulik's eyes as two of the Chinese courtesans,

(Sound of bare feet rhythmically shuffling on wooden boards.)

young, nude—this was really embarrassing, I had to look away, I mean, I am no prude, on the contrary, but what were these lovely young entertainers doing at the crematorium at the deathwatch of an ambassador?

VAN GULIK (amused):   Well, it wasn't really my idea but when I was peddling the manuscript of my first Judge Dee novel I ran into this Tokyo publisher, Tamaki-san I think his name was...Ah, there he is, how thoughtful to show up at my wake...

TAMAKI-SAN: Nude women are mysterious, they fit in well with mystery novels. You can draw them yourself, Your Excellency, in the Chinese Ming style, that you have mastered. The pictures will help sell your books. (laughs politely). Help distribute your erudite wisdom widely.

VAN GULIK: Nude women (he coughs), yes, you were right, Tamaki-sama. That is an excellent idea. *Arigato gozaimashta!* I will supply you with some interesting sketches. I spend much time studying the nudity of women. I am a great admirer of the feminine principle, Tamaki-sensei. Contemplating, researching and meditating on female nudity brings me closer to the goddess, she who provides all the answers, she who all men are waiting for...

TAMAKI-SAN: Kwannon-san? The goddess of compassion?

VAN GULIK: Yes, she sometimes calls herself that, but the attractive goddess can also be cruel.

TAMAKI-SAN: When she makes us wait, when we feel her divine presence but won't show herself, how cruel, yes when after encouraging us she doesn't appear at the appointed meeting place, doesn't fulfill our longing, yes...*Hama no matsukaze.*

VAN GULIK: The cool evening wind after a hot summer day. How did the poem go?

FEMALE VOICE: *Hama no matsukaze*
  Will she come? Will she come?
  I thought, while wandering along the beach—
  but there was nothing but the whispering wind
  in the pine trees.

(The Ch'in lute is being played.)

VDW: The erotic element of the quest. Van Gulik's nude ladies. Tamaki-san's goddess Kwannon whispering in the pine trees. In Daitoku-ji the monks wanted me to spend a few days in a room by myself. Meditating. They came to check on me from time to time, with the keisaku.

(WHACK! WHACK! WHACK! WHACK!)

VDW: My career was progressing I was being hit more often, harder too. For four days I had my legs folded up in that little three-mat room. Afterward I saw the teacher.

DAITOKU-JI ZEN MASTER: Did you concentrate? Did you still your mind?

VDW: What did they expect, these holy folks?

DAITOKU-JI ZEN MASTER: So what did you think about when you didn't concentrate.

VDW: Four days of torture and bad food. I had enough of the patient politeness, I knew some rough Japanese words by then. Fucking. That's what I had been thinking about. Inspired by Van Gulik's erotic tales caused by his publisher's fantasizing about the beautiful goddess Kwannon, I had been thinking about fucking and cunt. I told the Daitoku-ji teacher that. CUNT!

DAITOKU-JI ZEN MASTER (sympathetic, interested): Oh yes, fascinating subject, yes...cunt, the gate, the fluid gate, the fluid nothingness, the empty nothingness, we enter, we exit. (Dreamily, as he shakes his little handbell) Enter...exit. Enter...exit.

(Mozart's Requiem, Trudeliese Schmidt, mezzo-soprano, enters magnificently in the fourth movement and is joined by Margaret Price, soprano, Philips recording 411-420-2.)

VDW: The eternal female principle, discussed with a little old Zen master in a T'ang Dynasty Buddhist temple in Japan. Magnificent T'ang Dynasty architecture got wiped out in China, by the Red Guards, the destructive demons of the Cultural Revolution, that smashed most of Chinese antique art treasures, but in Japan the architecture was copied and kept. Japan preserved T'ang beauty.

(Sounds of footsteps in a long stone corridor, a creaking door, footsteps on a wooden floor)

There I was, in this ancient temple, trying to understand the great Void, to understand "das Nichts", but I was understanding nothing of nothing. Everytime I approached the idea of Nothing I found it too empty to even imagine. The Daitoku-ji teacher disagreed.

DAITOKU-JI ZEN MASTER: Void not empty. Nothingness is busy place. That is where all the Buddhas live.

VDW: How to find the Void? By walking the Tao? The way? But if you call it the way what you call it is not the way.

(Percussion imitating the sound of footsteps, a bamboo flute accompanies the seeker with eery notes.)

FEMALE VOICE: You can't say Tao exists,
 You can't say Tao does not exist,
 But you can find it in the silence,
 in wu-wei, in deedlessness.

VDW: So I find something—Van Gulik's teachings on the Orient—I find something worthwhile in doing nothing, by wandering about aimlessly within the silence of the deserted library of a monastery that disdains reading. I find Meneer Hendriks there, who solves Captain Uyeda's koan by giving up everything after fighting evil in his home town, in Amsterdam. Meneer Hendriks finally enters Nothing, in his miserable little room in a smelly lodging house when he pours boiling water into his dented tea pot. By that simple deed he manages to melt eternal snow on Mount Fuji. I also find Judge Dee in the Daitoku-ji library, in another Van Gulik book, the DEE GOONG AN, meaning "Dee's Famous Cases". "An" means case. The same "an" as in Ko-an. Ko-an means "public case." Koans are open to everyone. There is nothing secret about the maddening riddles. Even their answers are known. They can be looked up in textbooks. On the cover of the *De Goong An* book there's a naked lady drawn by Van Gulik himself. There's also Judge Dee, in his official robes, behind the bench.

(Mozart's requiem (just a little bit) - then Chinese court music - then Mozart again.)

Rudyard Kipling said: "East is East and West is West and Never the Twain will meet." What was Rudyard thinking of? Perhaps he meant that two sides of the same coin can't face each other. Observing Judge Dee and Van Gulik interact on the crematorium's stage it is sometimes hard to see who is who. I watch two tall men, both bigger than life: Dee in his regal robes, van Gulik in his three-piece suit, Dee with his flowing beard, van Gulik with his little round glasses. It seems their shapes keep joining, splitting up again, the one has features of the other, the other of the one. I remember that Ambassador van Gulik, at a party, gesturing with his long Cuban cigar and tulip-shaped jenever glass, said to his guests:

VAN GULIK (slightly drunk):   Judge Dee, that's *me*.

VDW: From their postures and gestures it seems clear that both men are superior, high ranking officials who sincerely attempt to serve the common good. Japan preserved Chinese T'ang Dynasty architecture. Van Gulik preserved T'ang wisdom and practicality in his writing. Judge

Dee, a real-life historical figure, started his career as a magistrate and finished it, at his death, age 70, as an all-powerful minister of state under Empress Wu. During Dee's lifetime there was much bad Buddhism going on.

(A big gong is sounded, chains are dragged across a stone floor.)

JUDGE DEE (bass voice with oriental accent): This court is now open. Corrupt Buddhist monks beware! Your greed, your womanizing, your pursuit of worldly power under the cloak of holiness, your fraudulent attempts at selling so-called enlightenment for services and goods, will not be tolerated.

VDW: Any method brings its own shadowside. I saw some of the Buddhist shadows in Japan. There was the organized Buddhist church, often mismanaged and exploited by self-serving priests enjoying perks that came with their high ranks. There were imported luxury cars, exotic mistresses, foreign vacations paid for by exorbitant fees charged for sutra chanting at the believers' homes, blessings, funeral services, promises of longevity, of divine insight, of eternal pleasures in heaven...

(The gong is sounded again, a gavel hits the bench.)

JUDGE DEE: All these crimes will be noted. Suspects will be arrested and charged, will kneel in front of this bench, face their magistrate who represents the all-powerful Imperial Court. Alleged criminals can be subjected to torture...

(These statements are supported by drum beats but now the Ch'in lute is heard again as the judge changes his tone of voice.)

Religion's purpose is liberation of ignorance, of alleviation of suffering, of living in harmony with the universe...

VDW: As a Zen student I am not supposed to read, but I keep sneaking into the monastic library to follow Dee's adventures. Dee is now also in contact with superior spirits, disguising themselves as hermits and tramps.

They are true Zen adepts who go beyond rules and regulations, who always renew their search, often well away from the confines of tradition. Men like cadaverous Master Gourd.

(Tones of Schubert's DEATH AND THE MAIDEN take us back to the funeral.)

VDW: It is getting crowded around Van Gulik's coffin. The mere mention of a name seems sufficient to summon another Van Gulik creation. Master Gourd comes in on his donkey. Gourd is old but, like Judge Dee, a tall wide-shouldered former athlete (I hear later he used to be an army general). The hermit sports a long beard. Seeing him bow to Van Gulik's coffin, and to the author himself, I remember reading how Dee, riding his beautiful horse through the forest, one misty day, meets the sage. Dee thinks he is facing a mirror, for in the fog the master's donkey looks like the judge's horse and the master's gourds, strung on each side of his donkey, resemble the judge's leather saddlebags. Dee, after a long day, hallucinating, too, is sure he is meeting himself. The experience is profound. Mirroring turns out to be the essence of Master Gourd's teaching method. Judge and Zen master ride on together and are attacked by bandits. Dee has to practise superior swordsmanship to stay alive but Master Gourd simply mirrors his opponents. Whenever a bad guy points a weapon the aged hermit mirrors the thrust with his walking stick, and parries the attack perfectly. The enemy, faced with the impossibility to slay his own mirror image, becomes exhausted, then flees. Later at the campfire, sharing a simple meal with the master, Judge Dee is curious.

JUDGE DEE: How did you do that, holy hermit?

GOURD (in a thin crackling voice): Empty yourself, become your opponent (laughs). But you're too full of being JUDGE DEE, you're an important official, so you have to work at survival, my dear. . .

VDW: Sly men, who call themselves unsui, clouds, who change their shapes, continuously appear and disappear.

JUDGE DEE: Are you a member of the Buddhist Church, Holy Hermit?

GOURD: Is a cloud a member of the sky?

VDW: But Judge Dee is a dutiful official—methodical, patient. . .

JUDGE DEE: I am impressed with your fighting method. I want to learn. You follow the Buddhist Zen method, Venerable Priest?

GOURD: Zen is only the finger pointing at the moon.

JUDGE DEE (flustered): But Zen. . .Buddha. . .

GOURD: Official, you know the Zen saying: "Buddha is dogshit?"

JUDGE DEE: But. . .but. . .

GOURD: Trying to hold on to this whole Buddha thing is a waste of time. Buddha is a statue made out of dogshit. You want to hold a filthy statue's hand? Let go, Official, let go. Empty yourself. There is nothing to lose. Tell me honestly, can you show me any eternal value in what you take for your precious body or soul. You only appear to be a person. (chuckles) Your ego never existed. Face the truth, official. Accept your true nature. Study the Heart Sutra (chants) -HAN-NYA-HA-RA-

MONKS (chanting):   -MI-TA-JI-SHO-KEN-GO-ON-KAI-KU-DO-

(As the monks chant we hear the cloppety clop of the donkey's hooves.)

VDW: Master Gourd has paid his respects and is leaving. Another Zen character takes his place. I'm pleased to recognize sacrilegious Sacristan Lu, a fat fellow who writes holy symbols on sheets with a broom. Judge Dee has heard that Lu is a wizard at mathematics. In one of Van Gulik's "Krimis" Dee respectfully approaches the uncouth Zen abbot and asks for professional help with a murder case the Judge is working on. Lu belches loudly without excusing himself.

LU: Don't you expect any help from me, Judge. I see human judgments as useless imaginations, and I won't raise a finger to help catch a killer. Murderers catch themselves. Run around in ever tighter circles. Fall over their own feet. They can't escape.

VDW: A great scene...an obese unshaven Buddha, resembling one of those statues in Chinese restaurants, staring at Judge Dee with "small bulging eyes", farting, scratching himself in the folds of his belly, dishing out free wisdom, daubing his giant Chinese characters on walls and roofs. Thanks to Lu I can surprise my own Zen teacher. In Van Gulik's book Lu talks about life and death. Lu lights a candle...

(Sound of a match being struck.)

LU: See the light?

JUDGE DEE: Yes?

(Sound of Lu blowing out the candle.)

LU: Where did the light go?

JUDGE DEE: Well...(hesitates)...well...

LU: Never mind.

(Sound of a match being struck.)

LU: Here is your light again.

VDW: I remembered that when my teacher blew out his candle and asked me where the light went. I flicked my lighter and brought the light back. A little show of Zen practicality. Why philosophize when we have the power to make light shine in the darkness, but my flicking the lighter did not explain why my schoolmates were taken to Treblinka.

GERMAN MAIDS (sing): Hoppa hoppa Reiter...

VDW: *Wenn er fallt ist er frei?* By letting go I overcome the duality of good and evil? The monastic teacher, *ushi no roshi* the monks call him, "the old man at home" tells us about a man dangling from a branch. Below snarls a tiger. Above him in the tree snarls another tiger. As the dangling man considers his position a white mouse and a black mouse come and gnaw on his branch. What to do?

LITTLE BOY (sings): *Wenn er fallt dann schreit er.*

VDW: Meneer Hendriks cries when captain Uyeda has him beaten, but then, long after Captain Uyeda is hung and long after Meneer Hendriks gives up trying to drown his sorrows in countless cold glasses of jenever, sipped in Amsterdam cafes, Meneer Hendriks stops crying. After bringing down Arab terrorists and saving a whore hooked on heroin he refuses the rewards due to any hero in any Krimi. How so? Because our hero no longer sees himself as someone who claims rights. His long sadhana, his arduous spiritual practice, has finally melted the idea of being separate. The "eternally frozen" ego is no longer there to be frozen. Illusionary good and evil mice can gnaw through non-existing branches of support as much as they like. . . having become nothing, nothing can touch his emptiness. As I see smiling Zen preacher Lu strutting around his author's coffin I see Lu's performance again in Van Gulik's novel. . .

(Chinese music clashing cymbals, shrieking violins, introducing. . .)

LU: Yes, my dears, I am a bodhisatva, a saint, an arahat, a superior man, a Buddha, who after a long and painful practise has reached the pinnacle of insight (he burps, says in a normal voice). . .boy, I should go a little easy on the pickled cabbage.

VOICES: (Laughing.)

LU (resumes his stage voice): Now then. . .you self-important folks, you who can't get enough of your interesting personalities, yes, like you there, Sir, you with the official hat and the flowing silk robe, and the long fingers caressing that huge lush beard. . .Judge Dee, is it? The famous magistrate? What do you have to say for yourself, Your Honor?

VOICES: (Laughing.)

JUDGE DEE (humorously): This unworthy servant of our great and glorious people puts himself at your bidding, Your Reverence.

LU (aside, casually): I like that, the narrow-minded Confucian scholar, the puffed-up so-called servant of the temporary people who wastes his energy on applying current morals ac-tu-al-ly shows a little respect for true knowledge (resumes his stage voice) look at me, whores and so-called ladies, beggars and pretending gents (he belches)(casual voice)...hah, that feels better...(resumes stage voice) you down there, the fearful people, you who worry about being and having, being more, having more, being less, having less, whenever you bother me in my temple it's always about the Two Problems, right? (uses pathetic voice) "Oh, almighty abbot, why am I so depressed, please make me feel better?" and "Oh, insightful teacher, what happens to me when I die?"

VOICES: (Laughing.)

LU: And to put me in a good mood you bring me all the goodies that interfere with my holy indigestion.

VOICES: (Laughing.)

LU: And I short-change you for I never seem to be able to come up with proper answers, well now...you living and suffering morons...(casual voice) it's the same thing you know, life, pain, what's the difference?...(resumes his stage voice) now, bring me a broom and put up a clean white sheet...good...a bucket full of black ink...hat's nice...thank you, you splendid fellow...here, I dip the broom in the bucket, and I-will-write-you -not an answer, no...

(He hits a big gong with a stick then quickly holds the gong to kill the sound.)

but a question, a symbol using my perfect

(Hits the gong again.)

free-for-all style

(Gong.)

my completely enlightened and detached void-filled champion calligraphy

(Gong.)

(Lu speaks casually now). . .here we go, folks here is the question that fully answers your questions. . .written nice and clearly, no teacher can write the truth any bigger.

(A swishing sound is accompanied by a bugle "blowing a circle.")

For those who can't read the little lady over there will be good enough to read my illustrious riddle, yes you, my pretty, there you go. . .

FEMALE VOICE: He just drew a circle.

LU: Thank you. Exactly right. I drew the circle that stands for your personal illusion. For each one of you. The circle that safely protects all that you think you are. What is your name, sir? You there?

IMPORTANT VOICE: My humble name is Mister Wang.

LU: *Mister* Wang. You're not so humble you know. You've put a big important circle around your Wang-ness. To hold on to all that self-importance. And you, little lady, what may your humble name be?

CUTE VOICE: My insignificant name is Fu.

LU: I beg your pardon. You're not so significant either. You're working hard on being an attractive little lady, aren't you? Don't you dress pretty! You must own a lot of finery and make-up on top of what you esteem as your natural beauty, and you've drawn a big fat circle around all your looks and paraphernalia so that nobody and nothing can take it away from you. Okay, last victim. You, Grandfather, what important seal have you stamped on that venerable white-bearded old sage's head of yours, huh?

QUAVERING OLD VOICE: People know this ailing old body as Dzjeng.

LU: Oh dear oh dear oh dear, so your circle holds all that age-old suffering together, does it? You want me to fix you up, grand-daddy of all grand-daddies? Be happy forever after?

QUAVERING OLD VOICE: Oh yes, please, Holy Abbot.

LU: I will I will. And you, Mister Wang? You want to be happy too?

IMPORTANT VOICE: I do, Reverend Sir.

LU: Very well very well, and what about you, beautiful dignified and attractive young Miss Fu? A big helping of divine joy for your eternal being?

CUTE VOICE: Oh yesssss...please...Buddha Lu.

LU: I will do that small thing. Now then, you, my friend, bring me that bucket filled with white paint if you please and help me show all you good people how simply all your imagined desires can be filled and al your so-called ills can be cured. Yes, hand me that broom.

(Sound of swishing, the bugle sounds again.)

There you go, my dears. No more circle, no more personality, no more humble *Mister* Wang who needs to puff up with wealth and fame, no more insignificant missy FU who needs to fill up her mirror with beauty, no more pathetic grand-daddy Dzjeng who has to keep his bag of brittle bones together.

ZEN MONKS (chanting): GO-ON-KAI-KU-DO-IS-SAI-KU-YAKU-SHA-RI-SHI-SHIKI-FU-I-KU-KU-FU-I-SHIKI-SHIKI SOKU-ZE-

(Chanting of the monks recedes and LU, who has a good singing voice chants the translation.)

LU: Form is not other than emptiness
and emptiness is not other than form.
Form is precisely emptiness,
and emptiness precisely form.

VOICES: (muddled mumbling)

LU: Think about it my dears, it's not hard to get. Be cool, be empty. Be Zero with the ring removed. Get it? No? You will, you will. And when you get it you don't only know what happens to you after death, will feel a-lot bet-ter!

(Sound of a gibbon, murmuring, then chanting.)

VDW: The stage is emptying out, only Van Gulik and Judge Dee remain, and above them, dangling from a beam by its long graceful arms, the gibbon Bubu. I know Bubu well for this intelligent being appears both in Van Gulik's novels and in his scholarly works. Van Gulik has much praise for these beautiful apes, who lived both in his gardens and houses.

VAN GULIK (coughs):   I allow my monkeys to go where they please. Animals are decent chaps, they never abuse a situation.

VDW: Van Gulik told me that a Gibbon is a primate, an intermediary between the animal and the human kingdoms. Gibbons walk upright, have no tail, behave themselves and will, unlike ourselves, only attack when cornered. Van Gulik's room mate Bubu peels fruit and offers it around before he eats himself. He uses a toilet and remembers to flush it. But there is more to a gibbon than superior ape-ness.

VAN GULIK: The gibbon was the traditional pure-Chinese symbol of the poet and the philosopher, and of the mysterious connection between man and nature.

VDW: The fifth century Chinese emperor Shen Yueh composes a poem.

FEMALE VOICE: The Wu mountains join each other
   for several hundreds of miles.
The River Pa weaves curve upon curve.
The flute's chant becomes louder, dies away.
The gibbons break their song
and start all over again.

VAN GULIK: Bubu died of influenza. When he felt his death coming he climbed to the top of the tallest tree in our garden and sat there quietly, with his long arms wrapped around his knees watching the sunset.

(Sounds of a duet, a ballad played on two seven-snared Chinese lute.)

VDW: As I said. It was a hot day. There were all those long boring funeral speeches going on. I must have closed my eyes for a moment. When, after listening to Judge Dee and Van Gulik play their lutes together, in a final duet before they left us to return to. . .

FEMALE VOICE: Where we all came from:
   where the flame goes when we snuff the candle.

VDW: . . .I reluctantly opened my eyes again. Even the coffin had disappeared, leaving the stage empty. I enjoyed watching the void and remembered the Datoku-jii Zen teacher:

DAITOKU-JI ZEN TEACHER: Void is very busy place. That is where all the Buddhas live.

VDW: All guests were served refreshments. I watched boiling water being poured into tea kettles as I faced the loneliness of a disciple who has said goodbye to his earthly teacher. But the abundant steam of the boiling water was helping to melt the eternal snow of Mount Fuji, as it had for Meneer Hendriks, who, like me, had been alone, just before he solved his ego-melting koan.

ZEN MONKS (chanting):   GYA-TEI-GYA-TEIHARA-SO-GYA-TEI-B0-JI-SOWA-KA-HAN-NYA-SHIN-GYOOOOOoooo...

VDW: The heart sutra sung daily in all Buddhist temples.

MONKS: When the bodhisatva was perfecting his understanding
and saw that all five existential levels are empty
he shouted out in joy
and immediately soared across all pain.

Meneer Hendriks, emptiness equals any type of taking shape
taking shape never was more than being nothing
and the same goes for feeling, seeing, willing, being there.

Meneer Hendriks, this no-rule neither came up nor went out
isn't impure, isn't pure
doesn't bring, doesn't take.

No shapes within the boundless void
no feeling, seeing, willing, being-there
no eye, ear, nose, tongue, body
no mind
no sight, sound, smell, taste, touch
no thing
there is no realm of the eye,
all the way up to no realm of realization.

There is no ignorance
and no ending of ignorance
through to no aging and death,
and no ending of aging and death
no pain, no cause of pain, no cessation of pain
and no path.

There is no wisdom or any attainment
with nothing to attain
saintly fellows relying on nothing whatever
have no hang-ups in their minds
having no attitudes
there is no fear
and departing far from confusion and imaginings
once and for all
bliss takes over.

All past, present and future free folks
relied, rely, will be relying
on awareness
of void.

Therefore know that nothingness
holds the great song of power
the great wisdom-producing chant
the supreme sacred chant
the unequalled holy humming
that dissolves all pains.

It is real and not false
therefore, recite the nothing-song:
gone, gone, gone beyond
gone completely beyond

HEY, YEY, SUPRAYEY,
EMPTY YEY,
FREE
FOREVER.